THE LIVING GOSPEL

Daily Devotions for Lent 2014

Theresa Rickard, O.P.

ave maria press  **notre dame, indiana**

© 2013 by RENEW International

Founded in 1865, Ave Maria Press is a ministry of the United States Province of Holy Cross.

www.avemariapress.com

Paperback: ISBN-10 1-59471-431-2, ISBN-13 978-1-59471-431-3

E-book: ISBN–10 1-59471-460-6, ISBN-13 978-1-59471-460-3

Cover image "At the Foot of the Cross" © 2012 by Jeni Butler, artworkbyjeni.wix.com.

Cover design by John Carson.

Text design by Kathy Coleman.

Printed and bound in the United States of America.

INTRODUCTION

God does not look at the caterpillar we are now,
but at the dazzling butterfly we have in us to become.

~Desmond Tutu

A caterpillar seems to have limited potential. But as it grows, it renews itself over and over by shedding the skin that can no longer contain it and growing a new one. When it has shed the last confining skin, the caterpillar retreats into a fragile shell, only to re-emerge in a glorious new life marked by color and flight. From its beginning, the caterpillar is destined for that new life; everything it does moves it closer to the day when it will spread its colorful wings and fly.

Archbishop Tutu used the development of a caterpillar into a butterfly to illustrate the transformation to which God has called each of us. Our response to that call is at the heart of Lent, a season when we devote time and attention to the call of conversion—the process of becoming our best and truest selves, the process of growing beyond the worldly things that burden us and taking flight in the freedom that comes only through friendship with God.

This conversion does not happen in a single day or during one season of Lent. We have moments of insight or elation and we have setbacks, such that for most of us, conversion is a slow movement forward. The goal of this gradual progress is what philosophers like the Jesuit priest Bernard Lonergan have called "self-transcendence." This is an ability to see the world as bigger than ourselves. This doesn't mean that we are insignificant, but rather that each of us has an indispensable part to play beyond our own pleasures, interests, and concerns.

Self-transcendence is the opposite of self-absorption—going through life thinking only of ourselves, our own security, convenience, and comfort.

Lent is an invitation to ask if we are stuck in place in self-absorption and to turn to Jesus as a model against which to evaluate our lives. His life was defined by generosity, self-sacrifice, and unconditional love for all people, not just his loved ones and disciples. We become the human beings God created us to be when we imitate that love. Lent is a time to pause and consider how far we have moved toward that ideal, to ask what may stand in our way, and to commit ourselves to taking even modest steps forward.

This small book can help you reflect on where you are in your movement toward God. Prayer and reflection on the daily Gospel readings can shake you from complacency and move you forward. Each two-page devotion for the days of Lent (Ash Wednesday through the Wednesday of Holy Week) includes brief prayers, a selection from the gospel reading of the day, a brief reflection, and an action step for spiritual growth. There are also shortened meditations for the most sacred days of the Easter Triduum (the "Three Days" that run from sundown on Holy Thursday through sundown on Easter Sunday), when we spend much of our time in church.

Try to spend at least five minutes with each day's devotion, at the same time and place if possible. You may want to use a bible along with this booklet so that you can read the entire gospel passage for the day. Citations for these are included each day, under the heading, **Listen.**

With God's help and through this booklet may you feel the Spirit stirring within you as you read and pray God's Word and turn it loose to spread its wings and grace the world.

Brothers and sisters:
We are ambassadors for Christ,
as if God were appealing through us.
We implore you on behalf of Christ,
be reconciled to God.

~2 Corinthians 5:20

MARCH 5
ASH WEDNESDAY

BEGIN

Spend a minute or two in silence. Set aside whatever might hinder your prayer.

PRAY

A clean heart create for me, O God, and a steadfast spirit renew within me.

~Psalm 51

LISTEN

Read Joel 2:12–18.

Even now, says the Lord, return to me with your whole heart, with fasting, and weeping, and mourning; Rend your hearts, not your garments, and return to the Lord, your God. . . . Blow the trumpet in Zion! Proclaim a fast, call an assembly; gather the people, notify the congregation.

~Joel 2:12

I Do Believe

I was giving a retreat on a university campus. In a faith conversation with a science doctoral student, she shared with me her struggle with the relationship between science and religion. As she came to a renewed faith in the person of Christ, she began to reconcile her deepening faith with her passion for science. She prayed for the courage and confidence to pursue her love for science while being a follower of Jesus Christ. A few weeks later she e-mailed me that, on returning to the lab after attending Mass on Ash Wednesday, she was tempted to wash off her ashes. Inspired by the words from the first reading, "return to me with your whole heart," she resisted and said a quick prayer to the Holy Spirit. Back at her lab station, one of her colleagues said to her, "Is that dirt on your forehead?" "No," she replied, "ashes; it is Ash Wednesday." Her colleague retorted, "You don't believe that stuff do you?" She responded, "Yes, I do believe!"

The external sign of ashes symbolized for my young friend her internal desire to personally and publicly give her life to the Lord. The mark of ashes was not about showing others she was good or religious; it was a way for her to profess her faith even at the risk of being ridiculed or discounted as a serious scientist. Our secular culture often makes it difficult for us to integrate faith into all areas of our lives. The Lord desires our whole heart—not just our heart on Sundays or our heart when we are among people with similar values and beliefs.

We commit ourselves during Lent to increase our giving to the poor, to prayer, and to fasting—not to impress others but to bear witness to our belief in Jesus Christ and his call to love God with all our hearts and our neighbor as ourselves. Even in these secular times— yes, even more so in these times—we pray for the grace to say, "Yes, Lord, I do believe!"

ACT

Take a step toward spiritual growth today.

I will contemplate what it means to wear a cross of ashes on my forehead. If at all possible, I will share my thoughts with someone else.

PRAY

Lord Jesus, give me the courage to witness to my faith in gentle and respectful ways. I pray for the grace to devote my whole heart to you through the power of the Holy Spirit. Amen.

MARCH 6
THURSDAY AFTER ASH WEDNESDAY

BEGIN

Spend a minute or two in silence. Set aside whatever might hinder your prayer.

PRAY

Choose life that you and your descendants may live, by loving the Lord, heeding God's voice and holding fast to him.

~Deuteronomy 30:19b–20

LISTEN

Read Luke 9:22–25.

"If anyone wishes to come after me, he must deny himself and take up his cross daily and follow me. For whoever wishes to save his life will lose it, but whoever loses his life for my sake will save it."

~Luke 9:23–24

Lose Yourself

I received an e-mail with "What is love?" in the subject line. It told the story of a teacher who asked her second graders, "What does love mean?" One response caught my attention: "When my grandmother got arthritis, she couldn't bend over and paint her toenails anymore. So my grandfather does it for her, even when his hand got arthritis too. That's what love is to me."

This simple response illustrates authentic love—the sacrificial nature of marriage that is no less than a "surrendering of one's life" for another. It is this kind of ordinary, everyday love that Jesus calls us to. The losing of one's life doesn't necessarily mean literally going to the cross, but any decision to chip off a bit of one's own life in order to give a bit of life to another.

Jesus revealed true love by losing his life so we may experience fullness of life now and in eternity. Lent is an opportunity to examine our lives in light of our decision to be followers of Christ. The cost of discipleship is losing ourselves in Christ's love so we may find our truest selves in loving others. It is the cross of sacrificial love that we chose to carry daily. It is the only path to life.

ACT

Take a step toward spiritual growth today.

Without complaint or resentment, I will do an ordinary act of love that has some personal cost to me.

PRAY

Lord Jesus, give me the grace to lose myself in you so I can become a more loving person. Help me choose each day to do the loving thing, no matter what it costs me, and so come to know abundant life in you. Amen.

March 7
Friday after Ash Wednesday

BEGIN

Spend a minute or two in silence. Set aside whatever might hinder your prayer.

PRAY

This, rather, is the fasting that I wish: Setting free the oppressed, sharing your bread with the hungry, sheltering the oppressed and homeless; clothing the naked when you see them.

~Isaiah 58:6–7a

LISTEN

Read Matthew 9:14–15.

The disciples of John approached Jesus and said, "Why do we and the Pharisees fast much, but your disciples do not fast?"

~Matthew 9:14–15

A True Fast

As a child, I thought Lent was about giving up things such as candy and fighting with my sister, Mary. I have come to realize true fasting results in inner conversion, and its fruits are outward signs such as just acts and charitable works.

The Gospel considers why Jesus' disciples eat while followers of the ascetic John the Baptist and other pious people fast. Jesus' response to his critics is that the wedding guest does not fast during a wedding. It would be like starting a diet on Thanksgiving. In other words, Jesus' historical presence and the ushering in of the reign of God is a time to celebrate, and the ritual of fasting is for another time.

Fasting is a beneficial spiritual practice anytime. It is especially helpful during Lent as we prepare for Easter. True fasting, devoted to prayer and charity, can transform us. The purpose of fasting is to help control our unruly selves for the sake of purifying our hearts and growing our capacity to practice charity. Fasting can help us surrender to God excess food or whatever else has undue power over us. It can help us let go of our compulsions and distractions so that these habits and material things can return to their rightful places in our lives. The fasting that Isaiah calls us to in today's first reading drives us from a life of selfishness or habit-driven living to one of generous giving and self control.

ACT

Take a step toward spiritual growth today.

I will carefully consider what I have chosen to give up for Lent and determine how the void created by my fast can be filled with what comes from God.

PRAY

Lord Jesus, your Word is the only food that will satisfy my hungry heart. Give me your grace to enter into a true fast this Lent. Through prayer and fasting, may my unruly self be refocused on your will and way. Transform my entire being and grow my willingness to practice charity. Amen.

March 8
Saturday after Ash Wednesday

BEGIN

Spend a minute or two in silence. Set aside whatever might hinder your prayer.

PRAY

God will renew your strength and you shall be like a watered garden, like a spring whose water never fails.

~Isaiah 58:9b–14

LISTEN

Read Luke 5:27–32.

"Why do you eat with tax collectors and sinners?" Jesus answered, "Those who are healthy do not need a physician, but the sick do. I have not come to call the righteous but sinners to repentance."

~Luke 5:30b–32

Here Comes Everybody

In his novel *Finnegan's Wake*, James Joyce wrote that the Catholic Church means, "Here comes everybody." In his blunt yet poetic way, Joyce captures our hope for the Church. At its root, the word catholic means all-embracing and wide-ranging—a church with room for all; a church where there is room for you and me.

This brief gospel scene is compelling because it describes not just the calling of one disciple, but Jesus' call to every person. Jesus moved through Galilean society, not handpicking the smartest and the purest, but instead the castoffs of society. The scandal of this scene in the eyes of the religious was that Jesus called forth a new community of disciples based on association with sinners rather than separation from them. Levi responds to Jesus' call in two ways: first, he leaves everything behind and follows Jesus; second, he throws a party for Jesus crowded with tax collectors. He does not give up on his friends, but instead draws them into the presence of Christ.

The good news is that we are all sinners called, redeemed, and healed by the love poured out in Jesus the Christ. The only ones excluded from God's reign are the arrogant who exclude themselves. When you are asked why you associate with the unwanted and unacceptable, you know you are continuing Jesus' work of building the kingdom of God.

ACT

Take a step toward spiritual growth today.

I will reach out in kindness to someone who seems to be lonely, hurting, or despairing

PRAY

Lord Jesus, transform me by the power of your Spirit so I may become your compassionate and welcoming presence to all. Renew your Church that we may become a true home for the unwanted, the lost, and the unacceptable. Amen.

Sunday, March 9
First Week of Lent

BEGIN

Spend a minute or two in silence. Set aside whatever might hinder your prayer.

PRAY

Give me back the joy of your salvation and a willing spirit sustain in me.

~Psalm 51:17a

LISTEN

Read Matthew 4:1–11.

At that time Jesus was led by the Spirit into the desert to be tempted by the devil. Then the devil left him and, behold, angels came and ministered to him.

~Matthew 4:1, 11

Finding God in Wilderness Times

Shortly after my dad died, my mom said to me, "Sometimes I look around this house in which I have lived for more than thirty years and I don't know where I am. I feel homeless." The loss of a loved one is one of life's crises that can throw us into a kind of wilderness experience, which can breed disorientation, loneliness, and vulnerability. A few weeks later, my mom remarked, "I don't know if I have the desire or the energy to begin a new life."

A wilderness journey is a time of testing, but also an opportunity to choose life in the midst of impending despair, or opt for God's way instead of the shallowness of immediate gratification. It is a time that takes advantage of our human weakness and opens us to temptation. But it also can be a time for growth.

We begin this first full week of Lent reading about the temptation of Jesus in the wilderness. He didn't choose the wilderness, but instead was led there by the Spirit. When the community Matthew was writing for heard about forty days in the wilderness, they immediately recalled the Exodus event. For the Israelites, the desert was not a success story—they failed the test and turned their backs on God. However, God remained faithful to them. Wilderness times test our faith as well, and challenge us to be transformed. My mom, through God's grace, eventually emerged from the desolation of grief. God sent angels to minister to her, and God will do the same for you.

ACT

Take a step toward spiritual growth today.

I will remember an experience of God leading me through a wilderness time and pray in gratitude for those who helped me through it.

PRAY

Lord Jesus, when I experience wilderness times, let me never forget God's unqualified mercy. As I face times of testing, give me the grace to choose life. Guide me through this Lenten season with a renewed desire to entrust my life into your hands. Amen.

BEGIN

Spend a minute or two in silence. Set aside whatever might hinder your prayer.

PRAY

Let the words of my mouth and the thought of my heart find favor before you, O Lord, my rock and my redeemer.

~Psalm 19:15

LISTEN

Read Matthew 25:31–46.

"Amen I say to you, what you did not do for one of these least ones, you did not do for me."

~Matthew 25:45

The Gospel of Love on Five Fingers

Mother Teresa instructed her sisters to remember the Gospel of Jesus Christ on five fingers. Holding up her fingers one at a time, she accented each word: "You-Did-It-To-Me." She then added: "At the end of your life, your five fingers will either excuse you or accuse you."

These words—"You did it to me"—come from the Judgment of the Nations (Matthew 25:31–46), in which Jesus tells us that we will be judged by how we treated those who were thirsty or hungry or sick. This passage makes it clear that when we respond with compassionate action to human need, we are responding to Christ. When we fail to respond, we are failing to respond to

Christ. We are called to be the church of Matthew 25, a community of committed disciples whose primary duty is to act with loving care for needy people.

What might we do this Lent to become the community of Matthew 25? Maybe instead of passing up rocky road ice cream, we will pass on the love of Christ by feeding our neighbors; instead of refraining from buying a piece of clothing during Lent, we will buy a set of new clothing for a needy person; or instead of giving up logging on to Facebook, we will log on to a worthy cause and make a donation. Be creative in your Lenten disiciplines, asking always what more you can do for those in need.

ACT

Take a step toward spiritual growth today.

I will reflect on the concrete actions of love and mercy described in this scene from the Gospel and do one thing today to help a person in need.

PRAY

Lord Jesus, give me the grace to have self-giving care for all my sisters and brothers, especially those in greatest need. Help me to say yes to the call to love, which is at the heart of the Father's will for me. Amen.

TUESDAY, MARCH 11
FIRST WEEK OF LENT

BEGIN

Spend a minute or two in silence. Set aside whatever might hinder your prayer.

PRAY

Glorify the Lord with me; let us together extol his name. I sought the Lord, and he answered me and delivered me from all my fears.

~Psalm 34:4–5

LISTEN

Read Matthew 6:7–15.

Jesus said to his disciples: "In praying, do not babble like the pagans, who think that they will be heard because of their many words. Do not be like them. Your Father knows what you need before you ask him."

~Matthew 6:7–8

Authentic Prayer

There is a Jewish tale about a poor farmer who discovered on the way to market that he left his prayer book behind. The wheel of his cart fell off so that he couldn't go back for the book, and it distressed him that the day would pass without him saying his prayers. So he prayed: "Lord, I have done something very foolish. I came away from home without my prayer book, and my memory is poor, and I can't recite a single prayer without it. So this is what I am going to do: I shall recite the alphabet five times very slowly, and you, to whom all prayers are known, can put the letters together to form the prayers I can't remember." And God said to his angels, "Of all the prayers I have heard today, this one was the most authentic because it came from a heart simple and sincere."

Matthew places Jesus' teaching on prayer at the center of the Sermon on the Mount, and the Lord's Prayer at the core of this instruction. In the Gospel, Jesus contrasts authentic prayer not only with the prayer of hypocrites in the synagogue, but also with that of the Gentiles whose practice of reciting many words to their pagan gods is empty and insincere. Some think that the way to get God's attention is to recite long and repetitious prayers or to pray in strict adherence to a formula. But Jesus reminds his followers that true prayer is simple and sincere. Prayer is about relationship, not duty. The heart of the Lord's Prayer, the model for all our prayer, is a resolve to commit our own will and action to fulfilling the will of God. Prayer isn't about manipulating God to do what we want; it's about humbly entrusting our troubles to a God who listens to our prayer and whose will is that we flourish as human beings.

ACT

Take a step toward spiritual growth today.

I will offer praise and thanks for this day and ask God to help me turn every joy into gratitude and every struggle into humble submission to his will.

PRAY

Loving God, I entrust this day to you. Give me a heart simple and sincere that is filled with a deep love for you and your will. I entrust myself to you this day. Lead me, guide me on the path of goodness and truth. In Jesus' name I pray. Amen.

BEGIN

Spend a minute or two in silence. Set aside whatever might hinder your prayer.

PRAY

A clean heart create for me, O God, and a steadfast spirit renew within me. Cast me not out from your presence and your Holy Spirit take not from me.

~Psalm 51:1–13

LISTEN

Read Luke 11:29–32.

While still more people gathered in the crowd, Jesus said to them, "This generation is an evil generation; it seeks a sign, but no sign will be given it, except the sign of Jonah. Just as Jonah became a sign to the Ninevites, so will the Son of Man be to this generation."

~Luke 11:29–30

God is Love

For seventy years, there had been a green neon sign proclaiming "God is Love" at a street corner in Florida. The sign was bent when a truck backed into it. Then the sign went dark for nine months when the house that supplied its electrical power went into foreclosure. Community leaders, philanthropists, and a sign business pitched in and repaired it. Many in the community testified that the sign caught their attention in their most difficult times and moved them toward God—although others hardly noticed the sign and still others scorned it. There are signs all around us that point to God—the beauty of a sunset, the roaring waves of an ocean, the birth of a baby, a spontaneous hug from a child, the care of a friend—if only we have eyes to recognize them. However, the greatest sign of God's love and presence is Jesus, the power and compassion of God.

After Jesus heals a man of an evil spirit and restores his speech, the people in the crowd have a variety of responses. Some say Jesus works by the power of the devil, and others call for him to give them a sign. His healing of the man is not enough for them. Jesus refuses to give them another sign but instead underscores his call for them to hear and obey the Word of God. In hearing Jonah's preaching, the people of Nineveh repent and change their lives, and yet the people in the gospel story refuse to hear and obey Jesus, the Word of God.

Lent is an opportunity for us to hear again Jesus' call to change our hearts and live according to the Gospel. Will we be like the crowd and ask for another sign, or will we follow the path of the Ninevites and repent of our selfish ways and follow Christ? No half-hearted response to God's unconditional love revealed in Jesus is sufficient.

ACT

Take a step toward spiritual growth today.

I will reflect on and name the signs of God's love and compassion in my life and commit to hearing and following Christ's word.

PRAY

Good and gracious God, open my eyes to the signs of your love today. Cleanse my heart, open my ears to your voice, and renew my spirit. Amen.

130:1–4

altar, and there
against you, leave
nd be reconciled
and offer your gift."

~Matthew 5:23–24

te in a small inner-city parish in
p of us gathered each day for Mass
ere were never more than ten of us.
chapel was Angie, and on the other
oth women were in their seventies and
is formerly Italian neighborhood their
hey never spoke. After a few weeks I found
y were sisters, and that they hadn't spoken in
ears because of anger over their mother's death
distribution of her personal items. I grew close

THURSDAY, MARCH 13
FIRST WEEK OF LENT

BEGIN

Spend a minute or two in silence. Set aside wh
might hinder your prayer.

PRAY

Lord, on the day I called for help, you ar
you built up strength within me.

LISTEN

Read Matthew 7:7–12.

"Ask and it will be given you;
knock and the door will be o
who asks, receives; and the
the one who knocks, the d

Another Door Opens

I can still hear my m
I was disappointed: "ᵥ
opens." Locked doors can see
even after repeated knocking that gᵣ
the door is unrelenting. Other times, our ᵣ
is rewarded; we finally hear footsteps and the
awaited turn of the knob as the door creaks open. W
breathe a sigh of relief.

In this section of the Sermon on the Mount, Jesus
concludes his instruction on how the disciples are to
live by encouraging them to pray—to ask, to seek, and
to knock. Knocking on the doors of mercy is a Jewish

FRIDAY, MARCH 14
FIRST WEEK OF LENT

BEGIN

Spend a minute or two in silence. Set aside whatever
might hinder your prayer.

PRAY

Out of the depths I cry to you, Lord; Lord, hear
my voice! Let your ears be attentive to my voice in
supplication. If you, Lord, mark iniquities, Lord, who
can stand? But with you is forgiveness that you are
revered.

–Psal

LISTEN

Read Matthew 5:20–26.

"Therefore, if you bring your gift to th
recall that your brother has anything
your gift there at the altar, go first
with your brother and then com

First, Be Reconciled

I was a pastoral associa
New York City. A gro
in a small chapel. T
On one side of th
side was Josie. B
had lived in t
whole lives.
out that the
twenty y
and the

to Josie, and she became the *abuela* of our small faith-sharing community of mostly young Latino mothers. It was hard for me to understand how this vibrant and loving woman could not forgive her sister.

When Josie had a pain in her leg, I took her to the doctor. Within a week, she was diagnosed with an aggressive tumor, and within months she died. Angie and Josie reconciled before Josie's death. During one of my last conversations with Josie, she said, "My one regret in life is to have wasted twenty years in bitterness and revenge against my sister. We missed out on so much of the goodness in each other's lives." Both Josie and Angie were committed to following Jesus, yet they found themselves in a bitter and unforgiving relationship. They were "stuck in place" and could not or refused to move forward.

In this Gospel passage, Jesus teaches his followers that they are to consider reconciliation and forgiveness even more important than worship at the altar. The God who is filled with compassion and forgiveness pours mercy upon us, inviting us, through God's grace, to do the same. Don't waste your life in bitterness; move forward in the freedom of God.

ACT

Take a step toward spiritual growth today.

I will place myself in the presence of the Lord and ask if there is someone in my life that I haven't been able to forgive. I will write that person's name on a piece of paper, keep it in the place where I pray, and ask God to show me a path to reconciliation.

PRAY

God of mercy and compassion, soften my heart toward those who hurt me. Give me the grace to practice the habit of forgiveness. Help me be like Jesus, the compassion of God. Amen.

SATURDAY, MARCH 15
FIRST WEEK OF LENT

BEGIN

Spend a minute or two in silence. Set aside whatever might hinder your prayer.

PRAY

Blessed are they whose way is blameless, who walk in the law of the Lord.

Blessed are they who observe his decrees, who seek God with all their heart.

~Psalm 119:1–2

LISTEN

Read Matthew 5:43–48.

"For if you love those who love you, what recompense will you have? Do not the tax collectors do the same? For if you greet your brothers and sisters only, what is unusual about that? Do not the pagans do the same? So be perfect, just as your heavenly Father is perfect."

~Matthew 5:46–48

The Perfection of Charity is Holiness

Ten years after Mother Teresa's death, the book *Come Be My Light*, which consists of letters to her spiritual director, was published. The letters revealed her deep doubt and despair as she strove to serve the God whose presence she could not always feel. The news media seized the moment and saw it as a great contradiction to the public persona of Mother Teresa. Journalists and others had assumed that Mother Teresa lived the life she did because she was perfect, or nearly so. However, they had it backwards. She lived a life of charity and sacrifice because she was in search of perfection, seeking and serving God in the midst of her struggles, doubts, and fears. That is what saints do, and that is the perfection we are called to.

Whatever our state or walk of life, we are all called to the perfection of charity. Mother Teresa explained that "in all of us there is the seed of something greater, the desire for holiness." If we love one another, she said, "we become holy. And if we are holy, then . . . people can look up and see only Jesus in us." Mother Teresa reminded her followers, "Holiness is not a luxury of the few but a simple duty for each one of us."

Many of us have trouble with the word "perfection." How can we be perfect? Jesus does not call us to moral perfection—an impossible ideal for us to obtain—or to perfection in the legalistic sense of keeping all the religious laws. The biblical word for perfection used in this Gospel passage means "wholeness." The perfection Jesus exhorts us to is to serve God wholeheartedly, to be single-minded in our devotion to God and in our striving to love our neighbor—not only our closest circle of friends and family, but also the stranger, and especially people who are most in need.

ACT

Take a step toward spiritual growth today.

I will be wholehearted today as Jesus asks of me and reach out in charity to someone who is outside my circle of family and friends.

PRAY

Lord Jesus, I place my weak and imperfect self before you and give you my life this day. Help me to live a life of charity and sacrifice in search of perfection, seeking and serving you in the midst of my struggles, doubts, and fears. Amen.

BEGIN

*Spend a minute or two in silence. Set aside whatever
might hinder your prayer.*

PRAY

Beloved: Bear your share of hardship for the gospel
with the strength that comes from God.

~2 Timothy 1:8b

LISTEN

Read Matthew 17:1–9.

Jesus took Peter, James, and John his brother, and led
them up a high mountain by themselves. And he was
transfigured before them; his face shone like the sun
and his clothes became white as light. And behold,
Moses and Elijah appeared to them, conversing with
him. Then Peter said to Jesus in reply, "Lord, it is good
that we are here."

~Matthew 17:1–3

Strengthened for the Dark Times

Fifteen years before my dad's death, he had a powerful
transfiguration experience, and it carried him through
the suffering he faced in the last months of life. My
parents traveled with a group to Mexico and visited the
shrine of Our Lady of Guadalupe. My father, a retired
New York City policeman and a faithful Catholic but
more salty than pious, climbed the steps and entered
the basilica. As he told the story, he left my mom and
her "cronies" outside the church "gabbing." Standing
in the back of the church, he listened to Mass being

celebrated in multiple languages. As the priest raised the host, my father experienced the overwhelming presence of God—he described a moment when all the people seemed to be holding hands as if they were one, and light emanated from the multi-ethnic congregation. He felt paralyzed, but he glanced at the woman next to him to see tears running down her face.

When my parents returned from Mexico, my father shared his mountaintop experience with many people, but eventually the story became a distant memory. However, during the last three months of his life, ninety-two years old and dying from cancer, he recalled this mysterious event. That memory strengthened him. My father, changed by his God experience at Guadalupe and strengthened by the memory of Christ's light, shouldered his cross and moved peacefully into the hands of a loving God.

God gave the disciples the transfiguration experience to carry them through the dark times to come. We will also be transformed when we share in the resurrection of Jesus. But that glory is already within us, for it does not come from the outside, but from the core of our beings.

ACT

Take a step toward spiritual growth today.

I will recall a time that I have experienced God's transforming presence in my life. I will write about it or tell my story to someone I love.

PRAY

God of light and compassion, I place my hope in Jesus Christ, who was transfigured before the apostles. I believe that I will share in that same glory. Strengthen me to face my own crosses and teach my heart to recognize the light of your loving presence. Amen.

MONDAY, MARCH 17
SECOND WEEK OF LENT

BEGIN

Spend a minute or two in silence. Set aside whatever might hinder your prayer.

PRAY

Remember not against us the iniquities of the past; may your compassion quickly come to us, for we are brought very low.

~Psalm 79:8

LISTEN

Read Luke 6:36–38.

Jesus said to his disciples: "Be merciful, just as your Father is merciful. Stop judging and you will not be judged. Stop condemning and you will not be condemned. Forgive and you will be forgiven."

~Luke 6:36–37

Stop Judging

I recently had a conversation with one of my older brothers about a woman I played basketball with in college. He chuckled as he reminded me how I used to complain to him, a basketball coach, about her. She was our star center, and for the first month or so of our season our tough coach allowed her to miss three out of six practices each week. I was indignant. I considered her a slacker. Years later, I found out that during that period her dad was sick and could not do all the chores on their farm. This "slacker" was getting up at four in the morning to milk cows and then go to classes and immediately return home to work the fields during the prime months of harvest. She worked all weekend while my friends and I frequented the pubs and worked at our social lives.

If we are honest, we know we judge others a lot, often with little evidence and even less compassion. Our media outlets are quick to condemn and slow to retract. We lack compassion for the weaknesses of others and ourselves. I always try to remind myself to not judge people's motives, even if their actions appear to be wrong. Jesus reminds us in today's gospel reading that the way of God is one of mercy and forgiveness. The more compassion we have for others, the more compassion we will receive.

ACT

Take a step toward spiritual growth today.

I will be mindful today of how quickly we judge others, in the media, in my interactions, and especially in my conversations. I will pray for a generous and more compassionate heart.

PRAYER

God of mercy and forgiveness, free me from my small judgmental ways and expand my heart to reach out to others in love. Amen.

TUESDAY, MARCH 18
SECOND WEEK OF LENT

BEGIN

Spend a minute or two in silence. Set aside whatever might hinder your prayer.

PRAY

Wash yourselves clean! Put away your misdeeds from before my eyes;
cease doing evil; learn to do good.
Make justice your aim: redress the wronged,
hear the orphan's plea, defend the widow.

~Isaiah 1:16–17

LISTEN

Read Matthew 23:1–12.

"Therefore, do and observe all things whatsoever they tell you, but do not follow their example. For they preach but do not practice. They tie up heavy burdens hard to carry and lay the on people's shoulders, but they will not lift a finger to move them. All their works are performed to be seen."

~Matthew 23:3–5a

Practice What You Preach

"Practice what you preach" has become almost cliché in today's world. However, there is an age-old truth contained in these words. A Gallup study found that only 12 percent of those who attend worship on Sunday showed evidence that their faith had any significant effect on their daily living—in terms of cheating on income tax, infidelity in marriage, lying, pilferage in business, and a variety of other spiritual, moral, and ethical issues.

We are not much different than some of the people of Jesus' day. I think there is an important reminder for us in the words of Jesus from today's gospel reading: our actions are to be consistent with our words. We go to Mass on Sunday, but is our conduct the other six days of the week consistent with what we pray and profess on Sunday? Each one of the new prayers at the conclusion of Mass begins with "Go." We are called to move from the Liturgy of the Word and Eucharist to the liturgy of the world. The object of our Christian faith is not to console us and make us feel good, but to exhort us to radically live the Gospel—proclaiming the kingdom of God first by our lives and then by our words. We are called, as St. Augustine reminds us, to become what we have received—Christ's love for the world.

ACT

Take a step toward spiritual growth today.

I will think about this past Sunday or the last time I went to Mass. Did I notice the words of dismissal at the end? I will try to live more faithful to the Gospel in all I do today.

PRAY

Good and gracious God, give me the strength to live in accordance with what I speak; give me grace to bear faithful witness, in word and in deed, to your glory and your grace. Help me to honor you with my lips, my heart, and my life.

WEDNESDAY, MARCH 19
SECOND WEEK OF LENT

BEGIN

Spend a minute or two in silence. Set aside whatever might hinder your prayer.

PRAY

But my trust is in you, O Lord; I say,
"You are my God."

In your hands is my destiny.

~Psalm 31:15, 16a

LISTEN

Read Matthew 20:17–28.

But Jesus summoned them and said, "You know that the rulers of the Gentiles lord it over them, and the great ones make their authority over them felt. But it shall not be so among you. Rather, whoever wishes to be first among you shall be your slaves. Just so, the Son of Man did not come to be served but to serve and to give his life as a ransom for many."

~Matthew 20:25–28

Mop Bucket Attitude

Dave Thomas, the founder of Wendy's, who died a few years ago, became a familiar sight to millions in his company's television commercials. One year, he appeared on the cover of his company's annual report dressed in a work apron with a mop and a bucket. Dave was a self-made man who didn't finish high school. He worked his way up through the ranks of Colonel Sanders's Kentucky Fried Chicken chain and from there founded Wendy's. Dave would often say, "I got my MBA long before my GED. At Wendy's, MBA does not mean Master of Business Administration. It means Mop Bucket Attitude." Dave Thomas taught all of his employees that service comes before success. The founder of Wendy's could have learned that lesson from Jesus. In the Scriptures, greatness is measured by service.

Jesus' vision of leadership is servanthood, and it corresponds to his alternative vision of kingship. Jesus does not use exalted and powerful terms to describe Christian leaders; instead he uses the word *diakonos* ("deacon"), which literally means "table servant." All followers of Jesus are called to Christian service wherever we find ourselves. If you will remind yourself at the start of each day that you are God's servant, interruptions won't frustrate you as much because your agenda will be whatever God wants to bring into your life. Remember, all your time—every moment—belongs to God. It is all right to have plans, but be ready and willing for God to upset them. Christian servants experience interruptions as opportunities to grow in patience and practice serving.

ACT

Take a step toward spiritual growth today.

I will keep in mind that my time belongs to God. I will reach out in service to someone beyond where my obligation lies. I will not expect anything in return.

PRAY

Jesus, you teach me by your word and life to be a servant of God. Help me see that greatness comes by humble service. Expand my heart and give me a servant's temperament—one that desires to serve others, expecting nothing in return. Amen.

Thursday, March 20
Second Week of Lent

BEGIN

Spend a minute or two in silence. Set aside whatever might hinder your prayer.

PRAY

Blessed the one who hopes in the Lord. He is like a tree planted near running water, that yields its fruit in due season, and whose leaves never fade. Whatever he does, prospers.

~Psalm 40:5a; Psalm 1:3

LISTEN

Read Luke 16:19–31.

"There was a rich man who dressed in purple garments and fine linen and dined sumptuously each day. And lying at his door was a poor man named Lazarus, covered with sores, who would gladly have eaten his fill of the scraps that fell from the rich man's table. Dogs even used to come and lick his sores. When the poor man died, he was carried away by angels to the bosom of Abraham. The rich man also died and was buried, and from the netherworld, where he was in torment, he raised his eyes and saw Abraham far off and Lazarus at his side."

~Luke 16:19–23

Look a Needy Neighbor in the Eye

An old Hasidic story tells of a congregation that thought they had a bright, innovative idea. They decided to put an end to the need for poor people to beg from door to door. They planned instead to put up a box into which wealthy people could drop their donations. Their wise rabbi put an immediate end to this alleged innovation, for he saw it for what it was. Hidden just below the surface was the desire to avoid looking a needy neighbor in the eye. The tendency to avoid people who are poor or disabled is a trait even among the most charitable.

In today's parable the rich man stepped over suffering Lazarus each day. Did he ever look Lazarus in the eye? I doubt it. Did he even notice the hunger and sores of this brother or was he too busy about his own life? This parable shocks us by showing very little mercy to the rich man who neither dressed Lazarus' sores nor fed his hunger. The rich man chose to serve mammon instead of God and, at his death, paid the consequence.

The parable clearly urges us to share food with the hungry, but even deeper than that, it insists we be good neighbors, especially to the most needy. True charity is more than giving a few coins to someone begging on a street corner, or writing a check to the local shelter at Christmas time. It is noticing, caring, and acting on the needs of our sister or brother—it is cultivating an attitude of the heart that suffers with our neighbor and compels us to respond compassionately.

ACT

Take a step toward spiritual growth today.

I will schedule a time to serve at a local care center before Lent ends. I will search my memory for any times I encountered someone in need and did not help, and I will seek forgiveness.

PRAY

God of compassion, give me a heart of mercy and care and a spirit of committed love. Graciously answer my prayer through Jesus, my brother and companion to the poor. Amen.

FRIDAY, MARCH 21
SECOND WEEK OF LENT

BEGIN

Spend a minute or two in silence. Set aside whatever might hinder your prayer.

PRAY

God so loved the world that he gave his only begotten Son; so that everyone who believes in him might have eternal life.

~John 3:16

LISTEN

Read Matthew 21:33–43, 45, 46.

Jesus said to them, "Did you never read in the Scriptures:

The stone that the builders rejected
has become the cornerstone;
by the Lord has this been done,
and it is wonderful in our eyes?"

~Matthew 21:42

The Cornerstone

A cornerstone is the foundation on which the entire building rests. A true cornerstone is firm and durable; its perfect form and peculiar position is the connecting link between the walls. It is not a stone you would want to stumble upon, let alone have fall on you.

Jesus responds to the religious leaders' lack of faith by telling three parables, one of which is today's gospel reading, the "parable of the bad tenants." These evil tenants refuse to pay the landowner rent, they reject and kill each of the landowner's representatives, and then finally they kill the landowner's son. Quoting from the Hebrew Scriptures, Jesus says, "the stone that the builders rejected has become the cornerstone." Jesus the Christ is the new cornerstone promised by God from the beginning of time to begin a new community centered on ushering in the reign of God. But he has been rejected.

One possible message for us as believers today is to see ourselves as the tenants or stewards of God's kingdom, charged with responsibility for producing good fruit—just acts and charitable works. We cannot produce this good fruit without choosing Christ as our cornerstone. Christ is the cornerstone upon which you want to build your life; he is your rock and refuge, and he calls you to align your values and beliefs with his will and way. Is Christ the foundation that holds up every facet of your life?

ACT

Take a step toward spiritual growth today.

I will begin a nightly examination of conscience. First, I will review my day, thinking about how God has blessed me. I will give thanks. Then, I will examine ways in which I have neglected to keep Christ as the cornerstone of my life. I will ask forgiveness.

PRAY

Loving God, thank you for sending your Son Jesus to be the cornerstone of my life. Give me the grace to build my life on the sure foundation of his teachings. Amen.

BEGIN

Spend a minute or two in silence. Set aside whatever might hinder your prayer.

PRAY

God pardons all your iniquities; he heals all your ills. He redeems your life from destruction; he crowns you with kindness and compassion.

~Psalm 103:3

LISTEN

Read Luke 15:1–3, 11–32.

"While he was still a long way off, his father caught sight of him, and was filled with compassion. He ran to his son, embraced him and kissed him. His son said to him, 'Father, I have sinned against heaven and against you; I no longer deserve to be called your son.' But his father ordered his servants, 'Quickly, bring the finest robe and put it on him; put a ring on his finger and sandals on his feet. Take the fattened calf and slaughter it. Then let us celebrate with a feast, because this son of mine was lost, and has been found.' Then the celebration began."

~Luke: 15:20–24

The Waiting Father

This well-known parable in Luke is most often referred to as the prodigal son. Helmut Thielicke, a German theologian, helps us to understand this story anew by retitling it, "The Waiting Father." Thielicke says the parable is not so much about a rebellious child as it is about a loving father who waits eagerly for our return. The word "prodigal" literally means "excessive," or "extravagant." When we're talking about the prodigal son, we are using the term in a negative sense. However, the word "prodigal" can mean "excessive" or "extravagant" in a more neutral or even positive sense. This is how it applies to the father in our story. He seemed to be recklessly extravagant in his love.

We may identify with either or both of the sons—the younger son who left home and was extravagant or excessive in the way he spent what had been given to him, or the older son who stayed home and was extravagant or excessive in his resentment and sense of entitlement. But the story is not all about us! It is about God as loving parent who not only forgives but also waits in loving anticipation for our return home into the compassionate heart of Christ.

Imagine God waiting with arms outstretched and running to meet you, inviting and cajoling you to turn away from your sinful ways, to let go of your unforgiving heart and commit to deeper Gospel love and living. How will you respond?

ACT

Take a step toward spiritual growth today.

I will ask the "waiting Father" for the courage to initiate reconciliation with someone I have struggled to forgive. I will first forgive, which is an act of the will, and then decide what next step I can take toward healing our relationship.

PRAY

Waiting Father, I thank you for your extravagant and reckless love for me. I open my heart and hands to your mercy. Amen.

Sunday, March 23
Third Week of Lent

BEGIN

Spend a minute or two in silence. Set aside whatever might hinder your prayer.

PRAY

Lord, you are truly the Savior of the world; give me living water, that I may never thirst again.

~John 4:42, 15

LISTEN

Read John 4:5–42.

Jesus answered and said to her, "Everyone who drinks this water will be thirsty again; but whoever drinks the water I shall give will never thirst; the water I shall give will become in him a spring of water welling up to eternal life." The woman said to him, "Sir, give me this water, so that I may not be thirsty or have to keep coming here to draw water."

~John 4:13–15

Drinking from the Well of Life

Years ago, I spent a summer studying Spanish in the Dominican Republic. I fell in love with the people and the beautiful countryside and even learned some Spanish. However, the water made me very sick. It looked and tasted fine, especially after I had been walking in the hot sun, but what I thought would quench my deep thirst was making me sicker and sicker. The parasites in the water wreaked havoc on my system. I lost twenty pounds and I ended up in the hospital for a week.

a loving father who waits eagerly for our return. The word "prodigal" literally means "excessive," or "extravagant." When we're talking about the prodigal son, we are using the term in a negative sense. However, the word "prodigal" can mean "excessive" or "extravagant" in a more neutral or even positive sense. This is how it applies to the father in our story. He seemed to be recklessly extravagant in his love.

We may identify with either or both of the sons—the younger son who left home and was extravagant or excessive in the way he spent what had been given to him, or the older son who stayed home and was extravagant or excessive in his resentment and sense of entitlement. But the story is not all about us! It is about God as loving parent who not only forgives but also waits in loving anticipation for our return home into the compassionate heart of Christ.

Imagine God waiting with arms outstretched and running to meet you, inviting and cajoling you to turn away from your sinful ways, to let go of your unforgiving heart and commit to deeper Gospel love and living. How will you respond?

ACT

Take a step toward spiritual growth today.

I will ask the "waiting Father" for the courage to initiate reconciliation with someone I have struggled to forgive. I will first forgive, which is an act of the will, and then decide what next step I can take toward healing our relationship.

PRAY

Waiting Father, I thank you for your extravagant and reckless love for me. I open my heart and hands to your mercy. Amen.

Sunday, March 23
Third Week of Lent

BEGIN

Spend a minute or two in silence. Set aside whatever might hinder your prayer.

PRAY

Lord, you are truly the Savior of the world; give me living water, that I may never thirst again.

~John 4:42, 15

LISTEN

Read John 4:5–42.

Jesus answered and said to her, "Everyone who drinks this water will be thirsty again; but whoever drinks the water I shall give will never thirst; the water I shall give will become in him a spring of water welling up to eternal life." The woman said to him, "Sir, give me this water, so that I may not be thirsty or have to keep coming here to draw water."

~John 4:13–15

Drinking from the Well of Life

Years ago, I spent a summer studying Spanish in the Dominican Republic. I fell in love with the people and the beautiful countryside and even learned some Spanish. However, the water made me very sick. It looked and tasted fine, especially after I had been walking in the hot sun, but what I thought would quench my deep thirst was making me sicker and sicker. The parasites in the water wreaked havoc on my system. I lost twenty pounds and I ended up in the hospital for a week.

The Samaritan woman in today's Gospel story had obviously been searching, and her search had led her to five different husbands, leaving her empty and bitter—that is, until the day she encountered Jesus at the well and received the water "welling up to eternal life." She left her water jar behind, returned to her village, and gave witness to her transforming encounter with Jesus.

For what are you thirsting? Where do you go to quench your thirst? To which wells are you drawn? There are many wells out there, but they often make us more thirsty or even addicted. There are the wells of superficial pleasures and quick fixes. Drinking from these wells satisfies us for only a moment, and often we are left numb and weak and thirsting for more.

When you are tired and feeling discouraged be refreshed and strengthened by Christ's Word; be fed by his body and blood so you can go forth and tell others about Christ's saving love.

ACT

Take a step toward spiritual growth today.

I will consider where I turn when I am in need of emotional or spiritual refreshment. Does this lead me to the Lord? If not, I will pray for courage to change the habits of my life so that my thirst is quenched by God.

PRAY

Jesus, source of living water, grant that I, who like the woman of Samaria thirst for living water, may turn to you as I hear your word and acknowledge the sin and burdens that weigh me down. In your gracious love, heal me. Amen.

MONDAY, MARCH 24
THIRD WEEK OF LENT

BEGIN

Spend a minute or two in silence. Set aside whatever might hinder your prayer.

PRAY

As the deer longs for the running waters, so my soul longs for you, O God.

~Psalm 42:2

LISTEN

Read Luke 4:24–30.

Jesus said to the people in the synagogue at Nazareth: "Amen I say to you. . . . It was to none of these that Elijah was sent, but only to a widow in Zarephath in the land of Sidon. Again there were many lepers in Israel since the time of Elisha the prophet; yet not one of them was cleansed, but only Naaman the Syrian." When the people in the synagogue heard this, they were all filled with fury. They rose up and drove Jesus out of town. . . ."

~Luke 4:24, 26–28

All Are Welcome

There was an article in the *Columbus Dispatch* about Jim Rush's garden. Usually backyard gardens are extensions of people's homes and are only for a small circle of neighbors and family. The opposite is true of Jim's garden. The sign in his front yard sums up his philosophy: "Garden is Open Please Stop In—All are Welcome," and people do. Jim believes a garden is to be shared.

it. There are signs all around us that point to God—the beauty of a sunset, the roaring waves of an ocean, the birth of a baby, a spontaneous hug from a child, the care of a friend—if only we have eyes to recognize them. However, the greatest sign of God's love and presence is Jesus, the power and compassion of God.

After Jesus heals a man of an evil spirit and restores his speech, the people in the crowd have a variety of responses. Some say Jesus works by the power of the devil, and others call for him to give them a sign. His healing of the man is not enough for them. Jesus refuses to give them another sign but instead underscores his call for them to hear and obey the Word of God. In hearing Jonah's preaching, the people of Nineveh repent and change their lives, and yet the people in the gospel story refuse to hear and obey Jesus, the Word of God.

Lent is an opportunity for us to hear again Jesus' call to change our hearts and live according to the Gospel. Will we be like the crowd and ask for another sign, or will we follow the path of the Ninevites and repent of our selfish ways and follow Christ? No half-hearted response to God's unconditional love revealed in Jesus is sufficient.

ACT

Take a step toward spiritual growth today.

I will reflect on and name the signs of God's love and compassion in my life and commit to hearing and following Christ's word.

PRAY

Good and gracious God, open my eyes to the signs of your love today. Cleanse my heart, open my ears to your voice, and renew my spirit. Amen.

Thursday, March 13
First Week of Lent

BEGIN

Spend a minute or two in silence. Set aside whatever might hinder your prayer.

PRAY

Lord, on the day I called for help, you answered me: you built up strength within me.

~Psalm 138:3

LISTEN

Read Matthew 7:7–12.

"Ask and it will be given you; seek and you will find; knock and the door will be opened to you. For anyone who asks, receives; and the one who seeks, finds; and to the one who knocks, the door will be opened."

~Matthew 7:7–8

Another Door Opens

I can still hear my mother's reassuring voice whenever I was disappointed: "When one door closes another opens." Locked doors can seem daunting. Sometimes, even after repeated knocking that grows into pounding, the door is unrelenting. Other times, our perseverance is rewarded; we finally hear footsteps and the long-awaited turn of the knob as the door creaks open. We breathe a sigh of relief.

In this section of the Sermon on the Mount, Jesus concludes his instruction on how the disciples are to live by encouraging them to pray—to ask, to seek, and to knock. Knocking on the doors of mercy is a Jewish expression of prayer. Prayer opens the doors of mercy, and God acts. Prayer is more about divine goodness than about human persistence; it is about relationship with God.

Some of my greatest accomplishments—periods of growth and learning—have begun with a closed door. Just as I heard my mom's reassuring voice, I hear the Lord reminding us today, "No matter what you face today, no matter how many closed doors you encounter, keep calling on the God who loves you for help and surety." We are encouraged to bring our needs to prayer, not in order to inform or change the way God acts in our lives, but to express our relationship with God as faith-filled disciples.

ACT

Take a step toward spiritual growth today.

I will recall a time when I felt deeply disappointed because a door had closed, but then found that another was open. I will give God thanks and extend my gratitude by encouraging someone else who is facing a closed door.

PRAY

Loving God, thank you for inviting me into a relationship with you and for answering my prayer with gracious and wise gifts. Bless me with a portion of your generous spirit so I may freely give to others wherever I find an open door. Amen.

FRIDAY, MARCH 14
FIRST WEEK OF LENT

BEGIN

Spend a minute or two in silence. Set aside whatever might hinder your prayer.

PRAY

Out of the depths I cry to you, Lord; Lord, hear my voice! Let your ears be attentive to my voice in supplication. If you, Lord, mark iniquities, Lord, who can stand? But with you is forgiveness that you are revered.

~Psalm 130:1–4

LISTEN

Read Matthew 5:20–26.

"Therefore, if you bring your gift to the altar, and there recall that your brother has anything against you, leave your gift there at the altar, go first and be reconciled with your brother, and then come and offer your gift."

~Matthew 5:23–24

First, Be Reconciled

I was a pastoral associate in a small inner-city parish in New York City. A group of us gathered each day for Mass in a small chapel. There were never more than ten of us. On one side of the chapel was Angie, and on the other side was Josie. Both women were in their seventies and had lived in this formerly Italian neighborhood their whole lives. They never spoke. After a few weeks I found out that they were sisters, and that they hadn't spoken in twenty years because of anger over their mother's death and the distribution of her personal items. I grew close

Jim's open and inclusive garden is like the kingdom of God preached by Jesus—all are welcome. Jesus is in his own town preaching and healing. At first, his neighbors are delighted to have a prophet in their midst. They consider it a great blessing until it becomes clear that Jesus is reading the scriptures differently. The hometown crowd interprets the scriptures to mean that God's kingdom is open exclusively to them. Jesus' philosophy is opposite—all are welcome to receive God's gracious love and blessings. Jesus leaves no one out. He connects his ministry to the prophets Elijah and Elisha; like them, he opens his ministry of deliverance and healing to those beyond the Jewish community. In fact, he welcomes the whole world in.

This gospel scene reminds us that God's grace cannot be fenced in like a private garden. It is not limited to the boundaries of any town, nation, church, group, gender, or race. The garden of God's love and healing power is open to all who enter in faith.

ACT

Take a step toward spiritual growth today.

I will examine the past week and ask if I have excluded someone unnecessarily, neglected to welcome another into conversation, or in other ways been inhospitable. I will consider how to change my attitude and learn to be more open.

PRAYER

Generous God, help me to expand my notion of community and welcome all kinds of people into my heart and life. Give me the grace to transcend the boundaries of community and the limits on love that I sometimes build. Amen.

Tuesday, March 25
Third Week of Lent

BEGIN

Spend a minute or two in silence. Set aside whatever might hinder your prayer.

PRAY

Your ways, O Lord, make known to me; teach me your paths, guide me in your truth and teach me, for you are God my savior.

~Psalm 25:4–5ab

LISTEN

Read Matthew 18:21–35.

"Lord, if my brother sins against me, how often must I forgive him? As many as seven times?" Jesus answered, "I say to you, not seven times but seventy-seven times."

~Matthew 18:21

Deep Gospel Living

On October 5, 2006, a troubled man barricaded himself in an Amish schoolhouse in the rural town of Nickel Mines, Pennsylvania. He dismissed the boys and shot ten of the girls—five were killed. The man later killed himself. Less than forty-eight hours later, the grandfather of one of the slain girls was standing next to his granddaughter's body as it was being prepared for burial. He said to a group of boys gathered around, "We must not think evil of this man." He urged them to forgive the killer. The community itself embraced the widow of the killer, inviting her to the funerals, telling her that she would be welcome to stay in their community. As cash donations from across the country began to pour in for the families of the victims, they insisted on sharing the money with her. This story of the Amish response to such a heinous act is a sign of God's amazing grace at work within a community: healing broken relationships, effecting harmony, creating peace, and restoring wholeness.

Peter's proposal to forgive seven times sounds incredibly generous. However, Jesus' response to Peter's proposal goes far beyond solely increasing the number of times to forgive. Jesus' pronouncement is about the nature of forgiveness—deep and radical Gospel living. Whoever counts has not forgiven at all. This kind of forgiving that reflects the deep Gospel living of the Amish community is beyond all calculation and is possible only through God's amazing grace. In Lent, we seek mercy and forgiveness from God. Let us be reconciled with sister and brother.

ACT

Take a step toward spiritual growth today.

I will write down the name of someone I have struggled to forgive, place the slip of paper in my hand and pray the Our Father. I will work all day at forgiving, letting go, and deciding on a path to mend the relationship.

PRAY

Merciful God, forgive me my trespasses and help me forgive those who have harmed me. Help me cling to the merciful and compassionate heart of Christ. Amen.

WEDNESDAY, MARCH 26
THIRD WEEK OF LENT

BEGIN

Spend a minute or two in silence. Set aside whatever might hinder your prayer.

PRAY

Your words, Lord, are Spirit and life; you have the words of everlasting life.

~ See John 6:63c, 68c

LISTEN

Read Matthew 5:17–19.

"But whoever obeys and teaches those commandments will be called greatest in the kingdom of heaven."

~Matthew 5:19

What is God Doing in Heaven?

When the question was posed, "What is God doing in heaven?", the rabbis customarily responded, "Reading Torah!" For Jews, the Law, or Torah, is a unique expression of God's plan for humanity and reveals God's inner thoughts. Jews relished the fact that God had given them the Law and they believed that this truth was evidence of God's personal and unique love for Israel. In scripture, laws are not presented as a burden, as rules to be obeyed for their own sake; rather, they are presented as our loving response to or acceptance of God's will for us.

Jesus was a faithful Jew and affirmed the fundamental goodness of the Law and the Prophets—the core of the Hebrew Bible. He reminded the disciples that he did not come to replace the Law but to fulfill it. However, this fulfillment did not always mean a mere continuation of the original law; it also meant moving beyond it or more deeply into it. Later in Matthew's Gospel, Jesus proclaimed that mercy, justice, love, and covenant fidelity were the weightier matters of the Law by which the rest was to be judged. For Jesus, obeying the law was not to agonize over every detail and scrupulously follow it, but to live its spirit—radically giving oneself over in love of God and neighbor.

Through the scriptures, Jesus urges us today to examine our lives and acknowledge when, in our inner thoughts and outward actions, we have ignored the call to love. Each day we have many choices to make; today, choose God's way of mercy, love, and justice so you will be truly great in the kingdom of God.

ACT

Take a step toward spiritual growth today.

I will reflect on how I make decisions about what is right and what is wrong, and I will pray that I always let the call of the Gospel be my guide.

PRAY

Loving God, help me to obey your law in the spirit of mercy, justice, and love. Infuse in me a new spirit as I struggle this day to choose love in my innermost thoughts and in my actions. Jesus, have mercy on me. Amen.

Thursday, March 27
Third Week of Lent

BEGIN

Spend a minute or two in silence. Set aside whatever might hinder your prayer.

PRAY

Oh, that today you would hear his voice: "Harden not your hearts."

~Psalm 95:7e–8a

LISTEN

Read Luke 11:14–23.

Jesus was driving out a demon that was mute, and when the demon had gone out, the mute man spoke and the crowds were amazed. Some of them said, "By the power of Beelzebul, the prince of demons, he drives out demons." But he knew their thoughts and said to them, "But if it is by the finger of God that I drive out demons, then the kingdom of God has come upon you."

~Luke 11:14–15, 17a, 20

Finger of God

The "finger of God" is a biblical phrase referring to miraculous acts done through God's power. Poetry, art, and film have explored this image, but it is most commonly discovered in ordinary life. We live in a world where God's fingerprints are found in the unlikeliest of places—if only we have eyes to see. When God's healing power touches the earth, it signals God's reign being ushered forth in our time.

In today's Gospel passage, Jesus drives out the demon from the mute man by the "finger of God." The man's voice is restored. Jesus' opponents accuse him of healing the man through the power of the devil. Jesus explains to the crowd that exorcisms show that Satan's power has been broken and, at the same time, that the reign of God is present among them. In this case, the expression "the finger of God" comes from Exodus 8:15, in which the Egyptian magicians explained Moses' signs and wonders to Pharaoh. The magicians declared to Pharaoh, "This is the finger of God." However, Pharaoh's heart was hardened, and he refused to listen to them. If Jesus' detractors understood as much as the Egyptian magicians did, they would also have seen that the kingdom of God was at hand.

How often do we recognize the finger of God working in and through us? How often do we stop to look?

ACT

Take a step toward spiritual growth today.

I will watch for the finger of God in the ordinary circumstances of my day and offer a prayer of thanks each time I see it.

PRAY

God of surprises, help me recognize your presence and power in my life every day. Help me comprehend that it is you tapping me on the shoulder and showing me the way. Soften my heart and open my ears so I might receive, listen, and act upon your word this day. Amen.

FRIDAY, MARCH 28
THIRD WEEK OF LENT

BEGIN

*Spend a minute or two in silence. Set aside whatever
might hinder your prayer.*

PRAY

But Israel I will feed with the finest wheat, I will satisfy
them with honey from the rock.

~Psalm 81:17

LISTEN

Read Mark 12:28–34.

"Which is the first of all the commandments?" Jesus
replied, "The first is this: Hear O Israel! The Lord our
God is Lord alone! You shall love the Lord with all your
heart, with all your soul, with all your mind, and with
all your strength. The second is this: You shall love your
neighbor as yourself."

~Mark 12:28–30

Love on Two Feet

St. Catherine was born in 1347 in Siena, Italy, the twenty-
fourth of twenty-five children. In her early years, she
wanted to live a contemplative life devoted to prayer,
but later she heard God calling her to an apostolic life.
Initially she resisted because she worried that her intimacy with God would diminish if she reached out to
her neighbor. God spoke to her heart, and she came to
understand that her care for others would be an avenue
for a greater expression of her love for him. How could
she walk with only the "one leg" of love for God if

she also did not walk with the "second leg" of love for God's people? Just as a bird cannot fly with one wing, she could not truly love the unseen God without giving herself in service to her sisters and brothers in need.

Catherine joined the Dominican *mantellate*, a community of lay women who served the poor and sick. At a time when social rules forbade a woman to leave her home unaccompanied by a man, Catherine traveled the streets of Siena alone, ministering to the sick and poor whom no one else would touch.

In today's Gospel passage, we hear the Great Commandment pressing us to walk on two feet—love of God and love of neighbor. The commitment to help our poorest sisters and brothers is not an option, but an expression of our love for God. The conversion that Lent invites us to is not only a turning away from sin and a turning toward God with single-hearted devotion, but also a turning toward our neighbor with a generous heart and empathetic spirit.

ACT

Take a step toward spiritual growth today.

I will do a random act of kindness as an expression of my love for God.

PRAY

Loving God, help me to imitate the way of St. Catherine, walking as a Christian disciple on two feet with a single-hearted love for you and a generous love of my neighbor. I ask this in the name of Jesus, the compassion of God, and through the Holy Spirit, the fountain of love. Amen.

SATURDAY, MARCH 29
THIRD WEEK OF LENT

BEGIN

Spend a minute or two in silence. Set aside whatever might hinder your prayer.

PRAY

Have mercy on me, O God, in your goodness; in the greatness of your compassion wipe out my offense. Thoroughly wash me from my guilt; and of my sin cleanse me.

~Psalm 51:3–4

LISTEN

Read Luke 18:9–14.

"The Pharisee took up his position and spoke this prayer to himself,

'O God, I thank you that I am not like the rest of humanity—greedy, dishonest, adulterous—or even like this tax collector. I fast twice a week, and I pay tithes on my whole income.' But the tax collector stood off at a distance and would not even raise his eyes to heaven but beat his breast and prayed, 'O God, be merciful to me a sinner.'"

~Luke 18:11–13

Mea Culpa

During a football game I was watching, a receiver dropped a would-be touchdown pass. He immediately fell to his knees, lowered his head, and beat his chest three times. This act of humility touched even a hard-nosed fan like me.

In today's Gospel parable, Jesus speaks of both the posture and prayer of a Pharisee and of a tax collector. The Pharisee separates himself from others in order to remain pure. He begins his prayer by addressing God and then continues in the first person. His prayer is all about himself and how righteous he is. He is aware of the tax collector in the temple and he regards him and others like him with contempt. As his prayer continues, he is absorbed and impressed with his own virtue and asks nothing of God. By contrast, the tax collector, who was often guilty of overcharging his neighbors, stands "off at a distance"— thereby acknowledging his unworthiness before God. He beats his breast as a humble sign of remorse and grief. His prayer echoes today's psalm, "Have mercy on me, O God."

This parable is not only about the proper posture for prayer but also speaks of the way the Pharisee regarded the tax collector. He totally disregards him. The Pharisee has lots of religious virtue and piety, but only judgment for his neighbor, the tax collector. Once again we hear the truth—only those who show mercy and forgiveness to others will receive mercy and forgiveness.

ACT

Take a step toward spiritual growth today.

I will be mindful of the areas of my life that need God's mercy and forgiveness. With courage and gratitude, I will open my heart and mind to those amazing gifts.

PRAY

Compassionate Father, have mercy on me, a sinner. Bless me with the virtue of humility and give me a heart full of mercy, especially for those I find difficult to love. Amen.

Sunday, March 30
Fourth Week of Lent

BEGIN

Spend a minute or two in silence. Set aside whatever might hinder your prayer.

PRAY

"I am the light of the world," says the Lord; "whoever follows me will have the light of life."

~John 8:12

LISTEN

Read John 9:1–41.

As Jesus passed by he saw a man blind from birth. . . .
he spat on the ground and made clay with the saliva,
and smeared the clay on his eyes, and said to him,
"Go wash in the Pool of Siloam" (which means "sent").
So he went and washed, and came back able to see.

~John 9:1, 6–9

Becoming Unstuck

I was living in a poor town called Eligido in the Dominican Republic. The family I was living with had electricity a few hours each morning and a few hours each night. I entered into the daily ritual of waiting for the light to come. The light came at a different hour each evening. As the light came to a particular block, the people would break out in cheers. You could hear the light coming before you could see it. I waited with anticipation as the light gradually came to our block, and then I joined in the cheering. The light coming to the town of

Eligido was a process, and it took time before the entire town was basking in light.

The powerful story of the blind beggar gradually moving from blindness to sight and then sight to insight reminds me that conversion, too, is a process. Jesus restores the man's physical sight, but that is just the beginning. After Jesus heals him, some Pharisees ask what he has to say about Jesus. He begins simply by calling Jesus a "man"—a wonderful person who did a great deed for him. Later, when asked again, he calls Jesus a "prophet." Then finally he professes Jesus as the "Son of God." Jesus, the light of the world, moves the man from blindness to sight and, more importantly, from sight to insight.

Lent is a good opportunity to reflect on your relationship with God. Are you growing in your knowledge of and closeness to God? Are you living the Gospel more deeply? If you are not moving forward spiritually, perhaps you are stuck and need to find a way to grow.

ACT

Take a step toward spiritual growth today.

I will recall a favorite memory of light scattering darkness and hold that imagine in my mind today as a reminder to thank God for the ability to move from darkness to sight to insight about his presence in my life.

PRAY

Jesus, you are the light of the world. Shed your light on me this day so I may come to know you more deeply. I do believe, Lord. Help my unbelief. Amen.

MONDAY, MARCH 31
FOURTH WEEK OF LENT

BEGIN

Spend a minute or two in silence. Set aside whatever might hinder your prayer.

PRAY

Hear, O Lord, and have pity on me; O Lord, be my helper. You changed my mourning into dancing; O Lord my God, forever I will give you thanks.

~Psalm 30:11–12a, 13b

LISTEN

Read John 4:43–54.

Jesus said to him "Unless you people see signs and wonders, you will not believe." The royal official said to him, "Sir, come down before my child dies." Jesus said him, "You may go; your son will live." The man believed what Jesus said to him and left.

~John 4:48–50

A Sign of Hope and Faith

Recently, a woman shared with me a story about a sign from God that her daughter received in a time of great need. Her daughter, a young mother with two small children, was diagnosed with stage-four colon cancer. Immediately before surgery, the surgeon shared with her the details of the operation. When he finished speaking, she asked him, "Do you pray for your patients before surgery?" He took out a pen, wrote on a small square piece of gauze, folded it, and handed it to her. She opened it and read, "For I know well the plans I have in mind for you—plans for your welfare and not for woe, so as to give you a future full of hope" (Jeremiah 29:11). She grasped the gauze in her hand, and she was rolled into surgery with a renewed faith and trust in God—the giver of all life.

Signs provide an opening to faith, but signs in themselves do not guarantee faith, nor is faith dependent on them. Jesus healed many people and performed powerful works, yet many still did not believe in him. In the incident described in today's Gospel reading, Jesus performed another sign and the royal official not only rejoiced in the miracle of his son's healing but also came to see beyond the miracle itself. When a miracle is fully understood as a sign, it points to who Jesus truly is—the giver of life—and Jesus points to who God is, and this is the ground for faith.

The young mother, like the royal official, saw beyond the sign and recognized the presence of Christ at her side. She did not go into surgery knowing the outcome, but she knew that God was with her and that all would be well. Instead of asking for a sign, ask for the grace to know the presence of God in ordinary human experience.

ACT

Take a step toward spiritual growth today.

I will think about the most difficult thing I face today and remember that God is with me and all will be well, no matter the outcome.

PRAY

God of healing and compassion, reveal to me your loving presence this day. Give me eyes to see and a heart open to your amazing grace. Increase my faith and help me to place my life into your tender care. Amen.

TUESDAY, APRIL 1
FOURTH WEEK OF LENT

BEGIN

Spend a minute or two in silence. Set aside whatever might hinder your prayer.

PRAY

God is our refuge and our strength, an ever-present help in distress. Therefore we fear not, though the earth be shaken and mountains plunge into the depths of the sea.

~Psalm 46:2–3

LISTEN

Read John 5:1–16.

When Jesus saw the man lying there and knew that he had been ill for a long time, he said to him, "Do you want to be made well?" The sick man answered him, "Sir, I have no one to put me into the pool when the water is stirred up; while I am on my way, someone else gets down there before me." Jesus said to him, "Rise, take up your mat, and walk." Immediately the man became well, took up his mat, and walked.

~John 5:6–9

Do You Want to Be Made Well?

Most of us are aware of the illness in our lives—physical, spiritual, or emotional. But we often don't like the cures, because remedies call for change. The doctor says, "You need to eat less fat, no salt, less sugar, and exercise," and we say, "I think I'll go get a second opinion." The counselor says, "You need to spend less time at work, more time with your family. Forgive and let go," and we say, "That sounds good. I'll get to that."

Like the man in the Gospel story who was lying at the healing pool for thirty-eight years, we have all sorts of excuses for avoiding healing in our lives, and we put up all sorts of defenses to prevent healing in our hearts.

What would it look like to be a whole, healthy, spiritually free person? What healing do you need in your life? Are you willing to step out in faith and ask for it? If a person is to be healed, she must first desire it. Jesus asked the sick man, "Do you really want to be healed?" The man replied, "Yes, but . . ." The sick man gave the excuse that there was no one to help him into the waters and that others jumped in front of him. Do these excuses seem familiar? Jesus told the man to do what he could not do—what he had tried to do for thirty-eight years. Jesus, the living water of God, commanded him to take up his mat and walk. On hearing these words, the man was immediately healed. He stood tall, picked up his mat, and walked.

Don't wait for your disease or your wounded spirit to bring you to death. Stand on your feet like a strong, spiritual person made whole! Become unstuck, move forward, and walk toward your Savior and your God.

ACT

Take a step toward spiritual growth today.

I will address one area of my life that needs healing and take a single step in that direction. I might call a doctor, research healthy eating, create an exercise plan, call a friend with whom I have an unresolved dispute, or seek help with financial problems.

PRAY

Lord Jesus, help me name my illness or distress and bring my desire for healing and wholeness to you. Open my heart to hear you say, "Rise and live!" Amen.

BEGIN

Spend a minute or two in silence. Set aside whatever might hinder your prayer.

PRAY

Can a mother forget her infant, be without tenderness for the child of her womb? Even should she forget, I will never forget you.

~Isaiah 49:15

LISTEN

Read John 5:17–30.

"For just as the Father raises the dead and gives life, so also does the Son give life to whomever he wishes. Amen, Amen, I say to you, whoever hears my word and believes in the one who sent me has eternal life and will not come to condemnation."

~John 5:21, 24

Loved into Life

Abandoned by her crack-addicted mother, Christine, who was born with multiple disabilities, spent her first two and a half years in hospitals. Eventually she was released to her grandmother's custody and was put in a corner of the living room and mostly ignored. Her grandmother referred to her as the "ugly one." Christine became non-responsive. At almost three years old, she entered foster care. Sr. Ursula became Christine's advocate and made sure that she was placed in a loving home and that she received every therapeutic and educational opportunity available. Christine's foster parents loved her unconditionally and nurtured her. She began to speak and interact with her new family, and her spirit gradually healed. Christine was loved back into life. Recently, Sr. Ursula told me Christine is always smiling, radiating life and joy to others. Her physical disabilities do not keep her from participating in a variety of activities and events with family and friends.

In the Old Testament, giving life is presented as a prerogative of God. In today's Gospel reading, Jesus claims the same authority as God the Father—the power over life and death. Sometimes we find ourselves spiritually dead. We feel unloved, and our spirit is flat. Jesus, who is the power of God, came to give us life. If you are dissatisfied with your spiritual vitality, give your life over once again to Christ, who loves you unconditionally and has the power to give you new life. We who have been loved into life by our God are called to extend that love to those who are regarded as unlovable. There are no "ugly ones" in the reign of God, only beautiful children of God.

ACT

Take a step toward spiritual growth today.

I will reach out with an act of kindness to someone who seems to be neglected, alone, or feeling lost.

PRAY

Loving God, you are the author of life. Thank you for your unconditional love revealed in Jesus and for never forgetting me, even when others do. Pour forth your mercy and compassion upon me so I may see and treat each person as one of your beautiful children. Amen.

THURSDAY, APRIL 3
FOURTH WEEK OF LENT

BEGIN

Spend a minute or two in silence. Set aside whatever might hinder your prayer.

PRAY

God so loved the world that he gave his only-begotten Son, so that everyone who believes in him might have eternal life.

~ John 3:16

LISTEN

Read John 5:31–47.

"I have testimony greater than John's. The works that the Father gave me to accomplish, these works that I perform testify on my behalf that the Father has sent me."

~John 5:36

Truth Is More Important Than the Facts

Frank Lloyd Wright, a famous American architect, once said, "The truth is more important than the facts." Jesus performed miracles on the Sabbath and thus was accused of violating God's law. The fact was that he did disobey the letter of the law, but his detractors could not see past that. It didn't matter to them that Jesus healed a man who was ill for thirty-eight years and gave him the power to walk—that was beside the point. A trial ensued and Jesus was condemned. Jesus defended himself by claiming his power and authority to work miracles on the Sabbath came from God. He pointed to the witness of John the Baptist, his own mighty works, and to God the Father. Jesus cannot be limited to acceptable Sabbath behavior. Yet many religious people could not see the gift of God in Jesus—they couldn't get past a broken law. The Sabbath laws were meant to give God honor and worship—to set aside all work in order to see God and his gifts more clearly. Instead, the Sabbath laws sometimes blinded some people to the healing power of God in Jesus.

We can also become overly caught up in rules and regulations and miss the spirit of the law. The greatest rule Jesus gave us is to love God and to love our neighbor as ourselves. All other laws come second to this great commandment. Fear, insecurity, and ideology can bind us to law and shelter us from wrestling with the fullness of truth in love. Are we missing a gift from God because we have condemned another or because we are blinded by strict adherence to a law?

ACT

Take a step toward spiritual growth today.

I will call to mind someone whom I have written off because he or she is not living as I think that person should. I will pray for that person, and ask God to show me Jesus present in that person's life.

PRAY

Compassionate God, give me the grace to follow your will and way. Help me to follow the spirit of your law of love and always give people the benefit of the doubt. Give me the courage to wrestle with the facts and always seek the fullness of truth in love. Amen.

Friday, April 4
Fourth Week of Lent

BEGIN

Spend a minute or two in silence. Set aside whatever might hinder your prayer.

PRAY

The Lord is close to the brokenhearted; and those who are crushed in spirit he saves.

~Psalm 34:19

LISTEN

Read John 7:1–2, 10, 25–30.

Some of the inhabitants of Jerusalem said, "Is he not the one they are trying to kill? And look, he is speaking openly and they say nothing to him. Could the authorities have realized that he is the Christ? But we know where he is from. When the Christ comes, no one will know where he is from."

~John 7:25–26

Speak and Live Courageously

Archbishop Oscar Romero of El Salvador was gunned down by his own government while celebrating Mass. On March 23, 1980, the day before his death, he appealed directly to the military and demanded that they disobey when ordered to kill their own people. In the eyes of his enemies, Romero had gone too far. He became a marked man. In an interview two weeks before his death, he said, "I have frequently been threatened with death. I must say that, as a Christian, I do not believe in death but in the resurrection. If they kill me, I shall rise again in the Salvadoran people."

In today's Gospel reading, Jesus is a marked man. He has infuriated both the religious and political leaders of his day and they have threatened his life. At first, Jesus did not go to Judea because he knew he was in danger. However, he later chose to put aside fear and go to Jerusalem for the Feast of Tabernacles and began teaching in the temple area in full view. Some people wondered if he was speaking freely because the religious leaders now believed that he really was the Messiah. The truth is that Jesus was teaching without fear because he was convinced that he had been sent by God.

We may not be marked men or women, but we also need courage to live and witness to our faith in secular society. We, too, have been sent by God to announce his presence to anyone who will hear us.

ACT

Take a step toward spiritual growth today.

Today, I will pray for the many innocent Christians all over the world who risk their lives as they go to church, open their businesses each day, or walk down the street. As time allows, I will research this issue and see how I might help spread the word about today's Christian martyrs.

PRAY

Gracious God, help me to stand firm in my faith convictions. Fill me with your courage and power so I may share your word by the testimony of my life and the truth of my words. I pray for those who risk their lives each day for the sake of the Gospel. Amen.

SATURDAY, APRIL 5
FOURTH WEEK OF LENT

BEGIN

Spend a minute or two in silence. Set aside whatever might hinder your prayer.

PRAY

Do me justice, O Lord, because I am just, and because of the innocence that is mine, let the malice of the wicked come to an end, but sustain the just, O searcher of heart and soul, O just God.

~Psalm 7:9bc–10

LISTEN

Read John 7:40–53.

Some of the crowd who heard these words of Jesus said, "This is truly the Prophet." Others said, "This is the Christ." But others said, "The Christ will not come from Galilee, will he?" So a division occurred in the crowd because of him.

~John 7:40–41; 43

Wrong Side of the Tracks

When I was teaching high school, I met a girl who lived in a beat-up trailer; many considered her to be from the "wrong side of the tracks." Her mother was an alcoholic and her father worked tirelessly to give her all that she needed. Annette was a bright girl, and I asked her if she was going to college. She replied, "No one gives someone like me a chance like that. They call me trailer trash."

The Pharisees in today's reading claimed that the working people in town were being led astray by this false prophet from Galilee. The Pharisees were frustrated that these common people did not know the law or the scriptures. If the people knew the scriptures, they certainly would not expect that the Messiah would come from this obscure place. Nicodemus tried to speak up to encourage his fellow Pharisees to open their minds and give Jesus a hearing, but they refused. They could not get beyond Jesus being from Galilee. The Pharisees were dead wrong about the true origin and identity of Jesus. Jesus was not from Galilee, nor was he simply a prophet; he was from God. Some of the people in my town were dead wrong about Annette—she was not from a trailer but from God—she was a child of God with promise and possibility.

Do you look down on people because they come from the "wrong side of the tracks" or from a country you know little about? Can you disregard the small town, the housing project, or any other circumstance that keeps you from seeing that each person comes from God and has the potential for greatness?

A C T

Take a step toward spiritual growth today.

I will recall someone I have considered being from the "wrong side of the tracks," and will ask God to forgive my blindness.

P R A Y

Lord, free me from prejudice and judgment of others. Give me the grace to see each person as a child of God with potential and promise, regardless of where they live or their place of origin. Give me the courage to stand up and advocate for those who are harshly and rashly judged because of external circumstances. Amen.

SUNDAY, APRIL 6
FIFTH WEEK OF LENT

BEGIN

Spend a minute or two in silence. Set aside whatever might hinder your prayer.

PRAY

I am the resurrection and the life, says the Lord; whoever believes in me, even if he dies, will never die.

~John 11:25a–26

LISTEN

Read John 11:1–45.

So they took away the stone. And Jesus raised his eyes and said, "Father, I thank you for hearing me. I know that you always hear me; but because of the crowd here I have said this, that they may believe you sent me." And when he said this, he cried out in a loud voice, "Lazarus, come out!" The dead man came out, tied hand and foot with burial bands, and his face was wrapped in a cloth. So Jesus said to them, "Untie him and let him go."

~John 11:41–44

Release Me, Lord, Unbind Me

Near the beginning of Mass, we pray the Penitential Rite, sometimes using the Greek version, "Kyrie, eleison. Christe, eleison. Kyrie, eleison." The Greek translation is powerful beyond its literal meaning: "Release us, Lord, unbind us." We also pray this in the prayer that Jesus taught us, the Our Father. Forgive us our sins as we forgive—or unbind us, as we unbind—those who trespass against us. In today's Gospel reading, Jesus calls Lazarus from the tomb to new life and invites his friends to unbind him and set him free.

As Jesus arrives at the tomb, burdened not only with his grief but also with the deep sorrow of Mary, Martha, and other friends who have gathered, he is deeply moved. In his grief, Jesus first thanks God, and then he calls Lazarus forth from the tomb. And Lazarus comes to life, bound by the wrappings of the funeral cloth. Jesus says to his friends, "Untie him and let him go." Lazarus lets himself be unbound.

We are often bound by sin and an incapacity or even unwillingness to forgive. Jesus waits for us in merciful love and tender compassion. He waits to set us free.

ACT

Take a step toward spiritual growth today.

I will identify two things from which I seek release, healing, or forgiveness. Imagining that I can hold these things in my hands. I will pray to open my heart and hands and let Jesus heal me.

PRAY

Lord, release me, unbind me, and let me go free. Amen.

BEGIN

Spend a minute or two in silence. Set aside whatever might hinder your prayer.

PRAY

Even though I walk in the dark valley I fear no evil; for you are at my side.

~Psalm 23:4ab

LISTEN

Read John 8:1–11.

"Let the one among you who is without sin be the first to throw a stone at her." Again he bent down and wrote on the ground. And in response, they went away one by one, beginning with the elders. Then Jesus straightened up and said to her, "Woman, where are they? Has no one condemned you?" She replied, "No one, sir." Then Jesus said, "Neither do I condemn you. Go, [and] from now on do not sin any more."

~John 8:7b–11

Begin Anew in Christ

A few years ago, there was international crossfire over Iran's stoning sentence for a woman convicted of adultery. A European Union official called it "barbaric," and an Iranian spokesman said it was about punishing a criminal—not a human rights issue. Many are unaware of the discrimination and violence against women that still exists today in many parts of the world, even our own. Some secular and religious institutions still uphold outdated attitudes toward women. Jesus challenged the establishment of his day, and we need to do the same.

Jesus told them, "Let the one among you who is without sin be the first to cast a stone at her," and then Jesus turned to the woman and said, "go and sin no more." Pope Francis reflected on this Gospel in a short homily: "I think even we are sometimes like these people who on the one hand want to listen to Jesus, but on the other hand, sometimes we like to stone others and condemn others. The message of Jesus is this: mercy." In a soft voice he repeated, "I say in all humility that this is the strongest message of the Lord: mercy."

The first one set free by God's mercy was not the woman, but the first elder to drop the stones from his clenched hands. Jesus shows us that even the most senior and honored members of the community are sinners. Jesus invites the woman to begin anew and to live as a free woman, not a condemned one. He brings the promise of freedom to all, but that demands a turning away from old ways and former beliefs.

ACT

Take a step toward spiritual growth today.

I will schedule a time to participate in the Sacrament of Penance by attending a parish reconciliation service or going to confession when it is available in my parish.

PRAY

Compassionate God, lead me on the right path. Give me the courage to speak up for the least in our society. Help me to turn from my sinful ways and toward your gracious mercy. Amen.

TUESDAY, APRIL 8
FIFTH WEEK OF LENT

BEGIN

Spend a minute or two in silence. Set aside whatever might hinder your prayer.

PRAY

O Lord, hear my prayer, and let my cry come to you. Hide not your face from me on the day of my distress. Incline your ear to me; in the day when I call, answer me speedily.

~Psalm 102:2–3

LISTEN

Read John 8:21–30.

So Jesus said to them, "When you lift up the Son of Man, then you will realize that I AM, and that I do nothing on my own, but I say only what the Father taught me. The one who sent me is with me. He has not left me alone, because I do what is pleasing to him."

~John 8:28–30

Look and Live

In today's reading from the Book of Numbers, the Israelites, newly freed by God from Egyptian slavery, complained about the lousy food and lack of water in the desert. God responded by sending them a plague of snakes. Many were bitten and died. Moses prayed and God relented. He told Moses to hold up a bronze serpent coiled around a staff and to instruct the people that if they looked up at the snake they would live. And that is what happened.

In the Gospel passage, Jesus tries convincing the religious leaders that he is sent from God. He tells them they will die in their sins unless they come to believe in him. Jesus points to the connection between the bronze snake being lifted up in the Book of Numbers and the way he will soon be lifted up on the cross. God used the hated symbol of Roman oppression—the cross—and turned it into the means of healing and salvation.

Look at the cross in a new way—as God's people looked at the snake in the desert. Face your sin and look for healing. Gaze at the cross and remember the sins of injustice, cruelty, and violence endemic in our world, but have faith in God's mercy for those who seek him. Next week, as you venerate the cross during the Good Friday liturgy, recall the sin in your life, but remember too that for Jesus and for those who follow him, the cross is not an instrument of death but the gateway to eternal life. God invites us to come to the cross of Christ and see, not only our sins, but Jesus, the one who has come to heal us of those sins and set us free. Look at the cross and live!

ACT

Take a step toward spiritual growth today.

If at all possible, I will commit to be at the Good Friday liturgy next week, rearranging my schedule as needed. I will learn about the service beforehand, if I do not already know what happens there.

PRAY

Suffering Christ, strengthen my belief in your redeeming work on the cross. Let me not turn from the evil in the world or rationalize my own sinful behavior, but look at you and live. Amen.

BEGIN

Spend a minute or two in silence. Set aside whatever might hinder your prayer.

PRAY

Blessed are they who have kept the word with a generous heart and yield a harvest through perseverance.

~John 14:6

LISTEN

Read John 8:31–42.

Jesus said to those Jews who believed in him, "If you remain in my word, you will truly be my disciples, and you will know the truth, and the truth will set you free."

~John 8:31

Do the Right Thing

Flight is a gripping film in which Denzel Washington plays a pilot named Whip, who miraculously lands a broken plane while he is drunk and high. He saves ninety-six of the one-hundred and two people on board. Throughout the film, he lies to himself and everyone else about his alcohol and drug abuse, refusing to accept responsibility for his actions. Finally, at a hearing, when it seems he will escape the truth and subsequent punishment, Whip admits not only that he was flying intoxicated but also that he is intoxicated at the hearing. Thirteen months later, an imprisoned Whip, serving a minimum five-year sentence, tells a support group of fellow inmates that he is glad to be sober and does not regret "doing the right thing," because he finally feels free.

In the gospel passage, Jesus makes three promises to those who commit to obey his word, "to do the right thing": they will be his disciples; they will know the truth; and the truth will set them free. The first two promises, his hearers accepted; but the third one, they resisted because it insinuated that they were not yet free. They argued with Jesus that they were the children of Abraham and never had been slaves to anyone. They were stuck on the literal meaning of slavery while Jesus reinterpreted slavery as being a slave to sin.

What are the sins that keep you from being free? What are the worries, bad habits, and attachments that may not be sinful but that keep you bound?

ACT

Take a step toward spiritual growth today.

I will review my life and bring to the Lord my worries, bad habits, and unhealthy attachments. I will humbly face the truth and ask God's to set me free.

PRAY

Jesus, you are the way, the truth, and the life. Heal me. Amen.

THURSDAY, APRIL 10
FIFTH WEEK OF LENT

BEGIN

Spend a minute or two in silence. Set aside whatever might hinder your prayer.

PRAY

If today you hear his voice, harden not your hearts.

~Psalm 95:8

LISTEN

Read John 8:51–59.

Jesus said to them, "Amen, amen, I say to you, before Abraham came to be, I AM." So they picked up stones to throw at him; but Jesus hid and went out of the temple area.

~John 8:58

Earth's Crammed with Heaven

Elizabeth Barrett Browning wrote a poem describing the scene when Moses, before going to face Pharaoh in Egypt, encountered God, self-described as "I AM," in the burning bush. She writes: "Earth's crammed with heaven, and every common bush afire with God; but only he who sees, takes off his shoes. The rest sit round it and pluck blackberries, and daub their natural faces unaware."

Moses knew that he was with God, but the Jewish authorities were totally unaware of the presence of God in Jesus. All the signs were there, but they refused to see. As Jesus' hour approached, the conflict between Jesus and the Jewish leaders heated up. It rose to the point of violence as they picked up stones to throw at Jesus. The heart of the conflict was about the identity of Jesus. He says, "I solemnly declare it: before Abraham came to be I AM." By using the phrase "I AM," Jesus clearly identified himself as one with God, his father, not Abraham. Abraham and Moses and all the great prophets rejoiced in the coming of Jesus, the fulfillment of the covenant. God who is utter mystery was made present in the person Jesus the Christ.

Earth is crammed with heaven, and God is present in our world. It is to this created world that God sent his only son, Jesus, not to condemn the world but to save it.

ACT

Take a step toward spiritual growth today.

I will be attentive to the presence of God in all that surrounds me today, and I will give God thanks.

PRAY

Jesus, you are the light of the world. Give me new eyes that I might be more aware of God's holy presence in my life this day. Amen.

Friday, April 11
Fifth Week of Lent

BEGIN

Spend a minute or two in silence. Set aside whatever might hinder your prayer.

PRAY

I love you, O Lord my strength, O Lord, my rock, my fortress, my deliverer.

~Psalm 18:2–3a

LISTEN

Read John 10:31–42.

"If I do not perform my Father's works, do not believe me; but if I perform them, even if you do not believe me, believe the works, so you may realize and understand that the Father is in me and I am in the Father."

~John 10:37–38

Are You Jesus?

There is a story told about a group of salesmen who rushed through an airport, kicking over a vendor's table and scattering apples all over the floor. The men continued on their way without even apologizing, but one of them stopped before boarding his plane and turned back. He found that the vendor was a poor young woman. He consoled her, helped her pick up the apples, and gave her some money to pay for the fruit that had been damaged. As he started to leave to change his ticket for a later flight, he heard the girl ask him: "Are you Jesus?" He looked back and thought for a moment before answering, "No, I'm not. Are you?"

In our Gospel reading for today, Jesus continues to challenge the Jewish leaders and tries to win their hearts, but they are so stuck on their understanding of scripture and tradition that they are closed to God's presence in Jesus' works. Jesus reminds them, "Many good deeds I have shown you from the Father. For which of these do you stone me?" Could it be for Jesus' works of preaching, healing, forgiving, praising God, caring for the poor, or reaching out to those on the margins of society? Many Jews listened to Jesus; they saw his good works and came to believe he was from God. But others ignored his works and couldn't get past their perception that he was blaspheming by making himself God.

Do your works reveal the Word of God in your heart? As Jesus revealed God, we are called to reveal Jesus to the world through charitable works, just acts, and kind hospitality.

ACT

Take a step toward spiritual growth today.

I will do a work of God for someone in need today.

PRAY

God of the poor and brokenhearted, give me the grace to reveal Jesus today by my loving words, patient responses, and kind actions. Amen.

Saturday, April 12
Fifth Week of Lent

BEGIN

Spend a minute or two in silence. Set aside whatever might hinder your prayer.

PRAY

My dwelling shall be with them; I will be their God, and they shall be my people.

~Ezekiel 37:27

LISTEN

Read John 11:45–56.

So from that day on they planned to kill him.

So Jesus no longer walked about in public. . . . Now the Passover of the Jews was near, . . . They looked for Jesus and said to one another as they were in the temple area, "What do you think? That he will not come to the feast?"

~John 11:53–54a, 55a–56

Worth the Risk

Since the Second Vatican Council, popes have been determined to exercise their role as pastors by having more direct contact with lay Catholics and many other people as well. Paul VI took this trend to a dramatic new level by visiting six continents and John Paul I, in his short tenure, demonstrated a desire to engage people directly. John Paul II traveled the world, making himself present to crowds of unprecedented numbers, and Benedict XVI also traveled extensively. Pope Francis, beginning on the day after his election, seeks to have face-to-face encounters with ordinary people. Risk is always involved when public figures step outside the ring of security; in fact, both Pope Paul and Pope John Paul II were the targets of assassination attempts. But modern popes have not been deterred by that risk any more than Jesus was deterred by the dangers he faced.

Religious leaders who were plotting Jesus' death asked, "What do you think? That he will not come to the feast?"—referring to the Passover observance in Jerusalem. Of course, Jesus went to the feast, and he was arrested and put to death. He had warned his followers that he would die, but also promised them that from his death would come salvation and eternal life.

When Jesus calls us to carry a cross, he doesn't mean that we necessarily have to accept a violent death, but we do have to be willing to give away our lives to others by being present to those who need love—to be Jesus in the lives of those around us. As you observe Holy Week, be aware of the many ways in which you can die for others by giving a part of your life to someone who needs it.

ACT

Take a step toward spiritual growth today.

I will work to be Christ's presence in my world today, especially where it feels risky to me. I will be bold and reach out to others in need, even if it's as simple as holding a door open.

PRAY

Lord Jesus, Savior of the world, as I prepare to walk with you during Holy Week, give me a courageous and expansive heart ready and willing to take a risk; to give away my life each day for others. Amen.

APRIL 13
PALM SUNDAY OF THE LORD'S PASSION

BEGIN

Spend a minute or two in silence. Set aside whatever might hinder your prayer.

PRAY

Christ Jesus, though he was in the form of God, did not regard equality with God something to be grasped. Rather, he emptied himself, taking the form of a slave, coming in human likeness; and found human in appearance, he humbled himself, becoming obedient to the point of death, even death on a cross.

~Philippians 2:6–8

LISTEN

Read Matthew 26:14–27:66.

The governor said to them in reply, "Which one of the two do you want me to release to you?" They answered, "Barabbas!" Pilate said to them, "Then what shall I do with Jesus called Messiah?" They all said, "Let him be crucified!" But he said, "Why? What evil has he done?" They only shouted louder, "Let him be crucified!"

~Matthew 27:21–23

Deeper Gospel Living

During World War II, Maximilian Kolbe, a Franciscan priest, sheltered Polish refugees, including about two thousand Jewish people. He was arrested and incarcerated at Auschwitz, a Nazi concentration camp. In July of 1941, a prisoner escaped and, in typical Nazi fashion, the officers picked ten men to be starved to death as a means of discouraging others from fleeing. One of the chosen was Polish army sergeant Franciszek Gajowniczek. Because Gajowniczek had a wife and children, Maximilian volunteered to take the sergeant's place. The Nazis agreed, and Maximilian and the other condemned men were consigned to a kind of dungeon where they languished. Maximilian Kolbe was killed by lethal injection and was canonized in 1982 forty years later.

Jesus rode into Jerusalem with the people lining the road, shouting his praises. A short time later, they were shouting for him to be crucified. Obviously their praise of Jesus as he entered Jerusalem was shallow—they possessed a casual, not a committed, faith. Maximilian Kolbe is a modern-day saint who shows us what it means to be a committed disciple of Jesus Christ. While Auschwitz, like Calvary, is a grim place that has been preserved to remind us of the worst possibilities of human behavior, it also memorializes the best possibilities by reminding us of what can happen when someone lives by the words of Jesus: "This is my commandment to you, that you love one another."

ACT

Take a step toward spiritual growth today.

I will give myself again to Christ by consciously making him the center of my life. I will follow his commands this day by sacrificing for the sake of another.

PRAY

Lord Jesus, fill me with a deep desire to live by your words to love others. Help me strengthen my commitment to be your disciple. Amen.

April 14
Monday of Holy Week

Spend a minute or two in silence. Set aside whatever might hinder your prayer.

PRAY

Here is my servant whom I uphold, my chosen one with whom I am pleased, Upon whom I have put my Spirit; he shall bring justice to the nations.

~Isaiah 42:1

LISTEN

Read John 12:1–11.

Six days before Passover Jesus came to Bethany, where Lazarus was, whom Jesus had raised from the dead. They gave a dinner for him there, and Martha served, while Lazarus was one of those reclining at table with him. Mary took a liter of costly perfumed oil made from genuine aromatic nard and anointed the feet of Jesus and dried them with her hair, the house was filled with the fragrance of the oil.

~John 12:1–3

A Mary Heart in a Martha World

My mom's favorite biblical characters were Mary and Martha. She said she longed to be Mary, sitting at the Lord's feet, but because of the busy demands of being a mother with six children and seventeen grandchildren, she most often found herself being Martha.

Mary and Martha are mentioned three times in the Gospels—hosting a dinner for Jesus; mourning the death and witnessing the raising of their brother,

Lazarus; and, in this account, hosting another dinner for Jesus shortly before his death. Each time, Martha is proactive, and in this gospel passage once again "Martha served," while Mary sat quietly attentive to Jesus, anointing his feet.

At both dinners, Jesus defends Mary. He tells Martha that "Mary has chosen the better part," and he tells Judas to leave Mary alone when Judas complains that she had bought expensive oil with money that could have been given to the poor.

Jesus comes into the midst of our busy lives, extending the same invitation he gave long ago to the two sisters from Bethany. Jesus invites us to choose the "the better part"—a joyful life of intimacy with him that flows naturally into loving service. All of us, Marys and Marthas alike, can draw closer to Christ: deepening our prayer life, strengthening our service, and doing both with less stress, more freedom, and spontaneous joy.

ACT

Take a step toward spiritual growth today.

I will spend at least fifteen minutes in prayerful reflection today. I will contemplate Jesus and my relationship with him.

PRAY

Loving God, help me to deepen my prayer life and strengthen my service, which flow from my love for you. Free me from judging myself and others, from resentment, and from trying to be someone I am not. Increase my joy in all I do. Amen.

APRIL 15
TUESDAY OF HOLY WEEK

BEGIN

Spend a minute or two in silence. Set aside whatever might hinder your prayer.

PRAY

In you, O Lord, I take refuge; let me never be put to shame. In your justice rescue me, and deliver me; incline your ear to me, and save me.

~Psalm 71:1–2

LISTEN

Read John 13:21–33, 36–38.

Reclining at table with the disciples, Jesus was deeply troubled and testified, "Amen, amen, I say to you, one of you will betray me." Peter asked him, "Master, who is it?" Jesus answered, "It is the one to whom I hand the morsel after I have dipped it." So he dipped the morsel and took it and handed it to Judas, son of Simon, the Iscariot. After Judas took the morsel, Satan entered him.

~John 13:21, 25–27

God Never Tires of Forgiving Us

In the poem "Richard Cory," Edwin Arlington Robinson describes the title character as wealthy, well dressed, and admired by all. The poem tells us that Richard Cory "fluttered pulses when he said, 'Good-morning,' and he glittered when he walked." The point of the poem is discovered in the lines, "We thought that he was everything to make us wish that we were in his place." The frightening and dramatic twist is delivered in the poem's final line: "And Richard Cory, one calm summer night, went home and put a bullet through his head."

On the outside, Richard seemed to have it all together, but inside he was obviously in the depth of despair. Like Judas, his dark despair cut him off from the truth of God's inexhaustible mercy.

The difference between Peter and Judas is that Judas, like Richard Cory, gave up on God's mercy. In contrast, Peter, who denied Christ three times, clung to faith. Peter had the capacity to experience God's mercy more than once. Judas could not move past his betrayal. No one is beyond redemption—not Peter, not Judas, not anyone. Pope Francis emphasized this shortly after his election last year. In one of his first messages, he said: "This is Jesus' message: mercy. On my part, I say it with humility; this is the Lord's strongest message: mercy. The Lord never tires of forgiving us—never! We are the ones who get tired of asking forgiveness."

There is nothing you have ever done or will do that will stop God from loving and forgiving you. We each have access to God's inexhaustible love through Jesus Christ, our brother and savior. Share it with the Peters and Judases in your life.

ACT

Take a step toward spiritual growth today.

I will search my heart for any unforgiven wrong that I have done or another has done to me. I will ask God to forgive me and to bless me with the courage to forgive myself and others.

PRAY

God of mercy and compassion, let me never tire of asking you for forgiveness. Pour your inexhaustible love upon me so my heart might be large enough to forgive those who hurt me. Renew my hope and cast out any despair that lingers in my spirit. Amen.

April 16
Wednesday of Holy Week

BEGIN

Spend a minute or two in silence. Set aside whatever might hinder your prayer.

PRAY

I will praise the name of God in song, and I will glorify him with thanksgiving: For the Lord hears the cry of the poor, and his own who are in bonds he spurns not.

~Psalm 69:31, 34

LISTEN

Read Matthew 26:14–25.

On the first day of the Feast of Unleavened Bread, the disciples approached Jesus and said, "Where do you want us to prepare for you to eat the Passover?" He said, "Go into the city to a certain man and tell him, 'The teacher says, "My appointed time draws near; in your house I shall celebrate the Passover with my disciples."'" The disciples then did as Jesus had ordered, and prepared the Passover.

~Matthew 26:17–19

Holy Preparation

Deirdre, one of my RENEW colleagues, shared at a staff retreat day during Holy Week that she is often distracted by the preparation needed to host her family and her husband's family for Easter dinner. The stress of shopping, cooking, and preparing her home occupies her mind. After we reflected together on today's reading about Jesus and his disciples preparing and sharing the Passover meal, Deirdre made the connection with her own Easter meal preparations. She told us that her action step in response to the reading was to bring a fresh and joyful attitude to preparing Easter dinner, offering all her preparation in loving service to the Lord and her family.

Today is the last full day of Lent. Tomorrow at sundown we begin the great "Three Days" or Easter Triduum, which stretches from sundown on Holy Thursday through sundown on Easter Sunday. The Triduum liturgies include several major services and can be properly understood as one continuous act of worship commemorating the passion, death, and resurrection of Jesus, so that we mark our own dying and rising of the past year. In today's gospel passage, we read about the beginning of preparations for the final events of Jesus' life on earth. He instructed the disciples to go to Jerusalem and get ready for the Passover meal. They immediately and willingly obeyed Jesus. They found an appropriate room in Jerusalem, removed any items that contained yeast, bought a lamb and had it ritually slaughtered, and made final preparations for an intimate Passover dinner with Jesus and his closest friends.

ACT

Take a step toward spiritual growth today.

Today and tomorrow are important days. Prepare generously and freely your heart, mind, and home for the celebration of Easter.

PRAY

Loving God, lead me into the Triduum with an open heart and seeking spirit. Give me a new heart and a new spirit as I enter more fully into the life, death, and resurrection of your Son, Jesus. Amen.

The Easter Triduum

These are important days to pray in church with your parish community. Meditations here are shortened in the hope that you can join in what happens there during these sacred days.

April 17, Holy Thursday

Listen

Read John 13:1–15.

So when Jesus washed their feet and put his garments back on and reclined at table again, he said to them, "Do you realize what I have done for you? You call me 'teacher' and 'master,' and rightly so, for indeed I am. If I, therefore, the master and teacher, have washed your feet, you ought to wash one another's feet. I have given you a model to follow, so that as I have done for you, you should also do."

~John 13:12–15

Jesus, Our Foot Washer God

During his inaugural Holy Thursday Mass, Pope Francis washed and kissed the feet of ten young men and two young women at a juvenile detention center in Rome. Speaking to the young offenders, Francis said that Jesus washed the feet of his disciples on the eve of his crucifixion in a gesture of love and service. In his homily the pope said, "This is a symbol, it is a sign. Washing your feet means I am at your service." He continued, "Help one another. This is what Jesus teaches us." His simple, loving action reverberated around the world.

The unlimited and unexpected love of Jesus bends before us, washes us clean, and urges us to treat each other—especially the least among us—with the same love. This day reminds us that the Gospel is a life to be lived and not just an ideal to be contemplated. Jesus sends us; will you go?

PRAY

> Lord Jesus, send forth your cleansing and healing love upon my entire being. Give me the grace to bow down before my sisters and brothers and imitate your love in humble service. Amen.

APRIL 18, GOOD FRIDAY

LISTEN

Read John 18:1-19:42.

Now Simon Peter was standing there keeping warm. And they said to him, "You are not one of his disciples, are you?" He denied it and said "I am not." One of the slaves of the high priest, a relative of the one whose ear Peter had cut off, said, "Didn't I see you in the garden with him?" Again Peter denied it. And immediately the cock crowed.

~John 18:25–27

Landing on Our Feet

A young boy visited a monastery with his mother. Approaching one of the monks he asked, "What do you do every day? The monk replied, "We fall down and we get up, we fall down and we get up, we fall down and we get up."

During the reading of the Passion, we hear the story of Peter vehemently betraying Jesus—his friend and

Lord—three times. Jesus courageously offered himself to those who came to arrest him, and he boldly responded to their interrogation. In contrast, Peter denied the one who so freely gave his life. But Jesus forgave Peter and restored him to full relationship. Jesus put Peter back on his feet.

Jesus, the great high priest, suffered in love to save us and set us free. He is present today wherever people are betrayed by their friends, accused falsely, treated unjustly, stripped of their human dignity, abused, or violated in any way.

Today, we remember that we are not alone on our journey through the sufferings of this life and that our journey is never without meaning and purpose. No matter how many times we lose our footing under the weight of our crosses, God always responds with mercy and sends a "Simon" to catch us, set us on our feet, and place us on the path of everlasting life.

PRAY

Merciful Lord, I put my life into your hands. Amen.

APRIL 19, HOLY SATURDAY

LISTEN

Read Matthew 28:1–10.

After the Sabbath, as the first day of the week was dawning, Mary Magdalene and the other Mary came to see the tomb. And behold, there was a great earthquake; for an angel of the Lord descended from heaven, approached, rolled back the stone, and sat upon it. The guards were shaken with fear of him and became like dead men. Then the angel said to the women in reply, "Do not be afraid! I know that you are seeking Jesus the crucified. He is not here, for he has been raised just as he said."

~Matthew 28:1–2, 4–6

Signs of Hope

I was living and ministering in a parish in the South Bronx, New York. It was a spring day, and I was walking alongside a vacant lot. It was filled with weeds, broken glass, and empty crack vials. I noticed something yellow, and as I stopped and looked closer, I was surprised to see three beautiful yellow daffodils pushing up against the weeds and debris. As they danced in the light wind, these hardy flowers were showing off all their beauty and glory in the midst of the strewn garbage. They were a bit bent and slightly scarred and yet full of hope and promise.

The women came to the tomb that morning bent over by grief and expecting only death. A sudden earthquake shook them out of their sorrow and awoke them to an angel announcing good news, assuring them: "Do not be afraid. Jesus is alive!" Like the women at the tomb and like those daffodils, we are scarred by our Good Friday stories of struggle, stumbling, and suffering. But we also give witness to the many kinds of resurrection that are just as real in our lives.

We are an Easter people called to embrace the cross always in the hope of resurrection. Many of us are bent and scarred and yet full of promise and hope because the tomb is empty, Jesus is alive, and he is with us.

PRAY

God of hope and promise, shake me from my sorrow and awaken me to your presence. Give me eyes to see and a heart attuned to resurrection happenings in my life. Amen.

April 20, Easter Sunday

LISTEN

The Lord is truly risen, alleluia.
To him be glory and power
for all the ages of eternity, alleluia, alleluia!

—*Entrance Antiphon*
Easter Sunday, Mass During the Day